Creation of the Modern Middle East

# Kuwait

Creation of the Modern Middle East

# Kuwait

Susan Korman

Introduction by
**Akbar Ahmed**
School of International Service
American University

**CHELSEA HOUSE**
P U B L I S H E R S
A Haights Cross Communications Company
**Philadelphia**

*Frontispiece:* A Kuwaiti man and woman in traditional dress—a long, white cotton robe for the man and a black cloak for the woman—are shown walking along the coast in the capital, Kuwait City.

CHELSEA HOUSE PUBLISHERS

VP, New Product Development  Sally Cheney
Director of Production  Kim Shinners
Creative Manager  Takeshi Takahashi
Manufacturing Manager  Diann Grasse

Staff for KUWAIT

Editor  Lee Marcott
Production Editor  Jaimie Winkler
Picture Researcher  Sarah Bloom
Series and Cover Designer  Keith Trego
Layout  21st Century Publishing and Communications, Inc.

A Haights Cross Communications ✦ Company

http://www.chelseahouse.com

3 5 7 9 8 6 4 2

Library of Congress Cataloging-in-Publication Data

Korman, Susan.
    Kuwait / Susan Korman.
        p. cm.—(Creation of the modern Middle East)
Summary: A history of the nation of Kuwait and a discussion of its role in the Middle East.
Includes bibliographical references and index.
    ISBN 0-7910-6512-X
    1. Kuwait—Juvenile literature. [1. Kuwait.] I. Title. II. Series.
DS247.K8 K67 2002
953.67—dc21
                                                        2002009602

# Table of Contents

# Index to the Photographs

# Creation of the Modern Middle East

Iran

Iraq

Israel

Jordan

The Kurds

Kuwait

Oman

Palestinian Authority

Saudi Arabia

Syria

Turkey

Yemen

# Introduction

Akbar Ahmed

The Middle East, it seems, is always in the news. Unfortunately, most of the news is of a troubling kind. Stories of suicide bombers, hijackers, street demonstrations, and ongoing violent conflict dominate these reports. The conflict draws in people living in lands far from the Middle East; some support one group, some support another, often on the basis of kinship or affinity and not on the merits of the case.

The Middle East is often identified with the Arabs. The region is seen as peopled by Arabs speaking Arabic and belonging to the Islamic faith. The stereotype of the Arab oil sheikh is a part of contemporary culture. But both of these images—that the Middle East is in perpetual anarchy and that it has an exclusive Arab identity—are oversimplifications of the region's complex contemporary reality.

In reality, the Middle East is an area that straddles Africa and Asia and has a combined population of over 200 million people inhabiting over twenty countries. It is a region that draws the entire world into its politics and, above all, it is the land that is the birth place of the three great Abrahamic faiths—Judaism, Christianity, and Islam. The city of Jerusalem is the point at which these three faiths come together and also where they tragically confront one another.

It is for these reasons that knowledge of the Middle East will remain of importance and that news from it will remain ongoing and interesting.

Let us consider the stereotype of the Middle East as a land of constant anarchy. It is easy to forget that some of the greatest lawgivers and people of peace were born, lived, and died here. In the Abrahamic tradition these names are a glorious roll call of human history—Abraham, Moses, Jesus, and Muhammad. In the tradition of the Middle East, where these names are especially revered, people often add the blessing "Peace be upon him" when speaking their names.

The land is clearly one that is shared by the great faiths. While it has a dominant Muslim character because of the large Muslim population, its Jewish and Christian presence must not be underestimated. Indeed, it is the dynamics of the relationships between the three faiths that allow us to enter the Middle East today and appreciate the points where these faiths come together or are in conflict.

To understand the predicament in which the people of the Middle East find themselves today, it is well to keep the facts of history before us. History is never far from the minds of the people in this region. Memories of the first great Arab dynasty, the Umayyads (661-750), based in Damascus, and the even greater one of the Abbasids (750-1258), based in Baghdad, are still kept alive in books and folklore. For the Arabs, their history, their culture, their tradition, their language, and above all their religion, provide them with a rich source of pride; but the glory of the past contrasts with the reality and powerlessness of contemporary life.

Many Arabs have blamed past rulers for their current situation beginning with the Ottomans who ruled them until World War I and then the European powers that divided their lands. When they achieved independence after World War II they discovered that the artificial boundaries created by the European powers cut across tribes and clans. Today, too, they complain that a form of Western imperialism still dominates their politics and rulers.

Again, while it is true that Arab history and Arab temperament have colored the Middle East strongly, there are other distinct peoples who have made a significant contribution to the culture of the region. Turkey is one such non-Arab nation with its own language, culture, and contribution to the region through the influence of the Ottoman Empire. Memories of that period for the Arabs are mixed, but what cannot be denied are the spectacular administrative and architectural achievements of the Ottomans. It is the longest dynasty in world history, beginning in 1300 and ending after World War I in 1922, when Kemal Ataturk wished to reject the past on the way to creating a modern Turkey.

Similarly, Iran is another non-Arab country with its own rich language and culture. Based in the minority sect of Islam, the Shia, Iran has often been in opposition to its Sunni neighbors, both Arab and Turk. Perhaps this confrontation helped to forge a unique Iranian, or Persian, cultural identity that, in turn, created the brilliant art, architecture, and poetry under the Safawids (1501-1722). The Safawid period also saw the establishment of the principle of interference or participation—depending on one's perspective—in matters of the state by the religious clerics. So while the Ayatollah Khomeini was very much a late 20th century figure, he was nonetheless reflecting the patterns of Iranian history.

Israel, too, represents an ancient, non-Arabic, cultural and religious tradition. Indeed, its very name is linked to the tribes that figure prominently in the stories of the Bible and it is through Jewish tradition that memory of the great biblical patriarchs like Abraham and Moses is kept alive. History is not a matter of years, but of millennia, in the Middle East.

Perhaps nothing has evoked as much emotional and political controversy among the Arabs as the creation of the state of Israel in 1948. With it came ideas of democracy and modern culture that seemed alien to many Arabs. Many saw the wars that followed stir further conflict and hatred; they also saw the wars as an inevitable clash between Islam and Judaism.

It is therefore important to make a comment on Islam and Judaism. The roots of prejudice against Jews can be anti-Semitic, anti-Judaic, and anti-Zionist. The prejudice may combine all three and there is often a degree of overlap. But in the case of the Arabs, the matter is more complicated because, by definition, Arabs cannot be anti-Semitic because they themselves are considered Semites. They cannot be anti-Judaic, because Islam recognizes the Jews as "people of the Book."

What this leaves us with is the clash between the political philosophy of Zionism, which is the establishment of a Jewish nation in Palestine, and Arab thought. The antagonism of the Arabs to Israel may result in the blurring of lines. A way must be found by Arabs and Israelis to live side by side in peace. Perhaps recognition of the common Abrahamic tradition is one way forward.

The hostility to Israel partly explains the negative coverage the Arabs get in the Western media. Arab Muslims are often accused of being anarchic and barbaric due to the violence of the Middle East. Yet, their history has produced some of the greatest figures in history.

Consider the example of Sultan Salahuddin Ayyoubi, popularly called Saladin in Western literature. Saladin had vowed to take revenge for the bloody massacres that the Crusaders had indulged in when they took Jerusalem in 1099. According to a European eyewitness account the blood in the streets was so deep that it came up to the knees of the horsemen.

Yet, when Saladin took Jerusalem in 1187, he showed the essential compassion and tolerance that is at the heart of the Abrahamic faiths. He not only released the prisoners after ransom, as was the custom, but paid for those who were too poor to afford any ransom. His nobles and commanders were furious that he had not taken a bloody revenge. Saladin is still remembered in the bazaars and villages as a leader of great learning and compassion. When contemporary leaders are compared to Saladin, they are usually found wanting. One reason may be that the problems of the region are daunting.

The Middle East faces three major problems that will need solutions in the twenty-first century. These problems affect society and politics and need to be tackled by the rulers in those lands and all other people interested in creating a degree of dialogue and participation.

The first of the problems is that of democracy. Although democracy is practiced in some form in a number of the Arab countries, for the majority of ordinary people there is little sense of participation in their government. The frustration of helplessness in the face of an indifferent bureaucracy at the lower levels of administration is easily converted to violence. The indifference of the state to the pressing needs of the "street" means that other non-governmental organizations can step in. Islamic organizations offering health and education programs to people in the shantytowns and villages have therefore emerged and flourished over the last decades.

The lack of democracy also means that the ruler becomes remote and autocratic over time as he consolidates his power. It is not uncommon for many rulers in the Middle East to pass on their rule to their son. Dynastic rule, whether kingly or based in a dictatorship, excludes ordinary people from a sense of participation in their own governance. They need to feel empowered. Muslims need to feel that they are able to participate in the process of government. They must feel that they are able to elect their leaders into office and if these leaders do not deliver on their promises, that they can throw them out. Too many of the rulers are nasty and brutish. Too many Muslim leaders are kings and military dictators. Many of them ensure that their sons or relatives stay on to perpetuate their dynastic rule.

With democracy, Muslim peoples will be able to better bridge the gaps that are widening between the rich and the poor. The sight of palatial mansions with security guards carrying automatic weapons standing outside them and, alongside, hovels teeming with starkly poor children is a common one in Muslim cities. The distribution of wealth must remain a priority of any democratic government.

The second problem in the Middle East that has wide ramifications in society is that of education. Although Islam emphasizes knowledge and learning, the sad reality is that the standards of education are unsatisfactory. In addition, the climate for scholarship and intellectual activity is discouraging. Scholars are too often silenced, jailed, or chased out of the country by the administration. The sycophants and the intelligence services whose only aim is to tell the ruler what he would like to hear, fill the vacuum.

Education needs to be vigorously reformed. The *madrassah,* or religious school, which is the institution that provides primary education for millions of boys in the Middle East, needs to be brought into line with the more prestigious Westernized schools reserved for the elite of the land. By allowing two distinct streams of education to develop, Muslim nations are encouraging the growth of two separate societies: a largely illiterate and frustrated population that is susceptible to leaders with simple answers to the world's problems and a small, Westernized, often corrupt and usually uncaring group of elite. The third problem facing the Middle East is that of representation in the mass media. Although this point is hard to pin down, the images in the media are creating problems of understanding and communication in the communities living in the Middle East. Muslims, for example, will always complain that they are depicted in negative stereotypes in the non-Arab media. The result of the media onslaught that plagues Muslims is the sense of anger on the one hand and the feeling of loss of dignity on the other. Few Muslims will discuss the media rationally. Greater Muslim participation in the media and greater interaction will help to solve the problem. But it is not so simple. The Israelis also complain of the stereotypes in the Arab media that depict them negatively.

Muslims are aware that their religious culture represents a civilization rich in compassion and tolerance. They are aware that given a period of stability in which they can grapple with the problems of democracy, education, and self-image they can take their rightful place in the community of nations. However painful the current reality, they do carry an idea of an ideal human society with them. Whether a Turk, or an Iranian, or an Arab, every Muslim is aware of the message that the prophet of Islam brought to this region in the seventh century. This message still has resonance for these societies. Here are words from the last address of the prophet spoken to his people:

> All of you descend from Adam and Adam was made of earth. There is no superiority for an Arab over a non-Arab nor for a non-Arab over an Arab, neither for a white man over a black man nor a black man over a white man . . . the noblest among you is the one who is most deeply conscious of God.

This is a noble and worthy message for the twenty-first century in the Middle East. Not only Muslims, but Jews, and Christians would agree with it. Perhaps its essential theme of tolerance, compassion, and equality can help to rediscover the wellsprings of tradition that can both inspire and unite.

It is for these reasons that I congratulate Chelsea House Publishers for taking the initiative in helping us to understand the Middle East through this series. The story of the Middle East is, in many profound ways, the story of human civilization.

— **Dr. Akbar S. Ahmed**
**The Ibn Khaldun Chair of Islamic Studies and**
**Professor of International Relations,**
**School of International Service**
**American University**

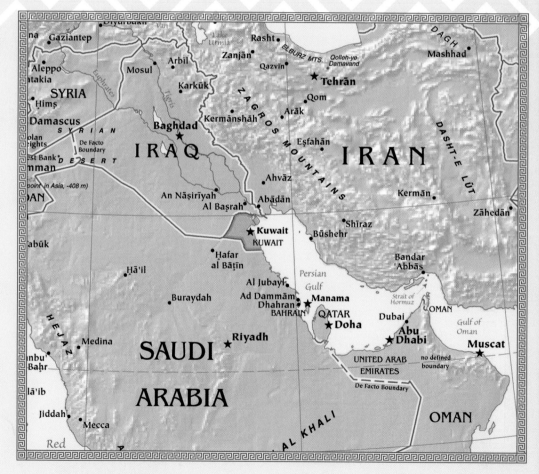

Kuwait in the Middle East region

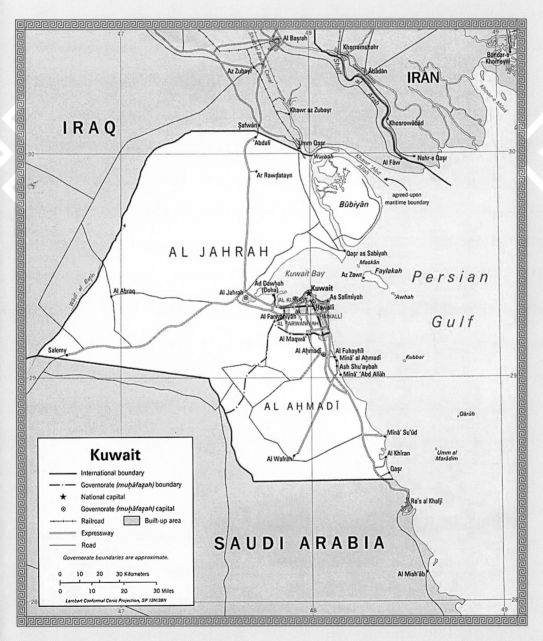

Modern map of Kuwait

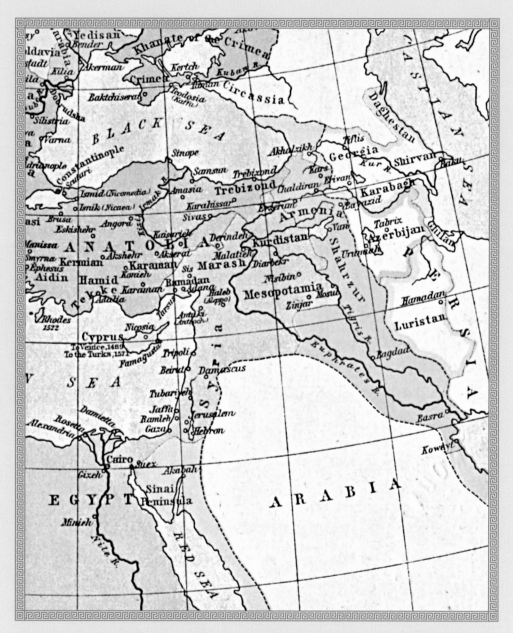

This map of the Ottoman Empire shows Kuwait (Koweyt) in the lower right-hand corner. The Ottomans dominated Kuwait during the reign of the first al-Sabah sheik in the 1750s.

# 1

# Kuwait, 1896

I t was just before midnight on May 8, 1896, when Mubarak al-Sabah rode on camelback across the desert. He was on his way to the palace of the sheik, or ruler, of Kuwait. With him was a band of followers, which included two of his sons. It was pitch-black outside, but Mubarak had chosen to make his trek in darkness for a very specific reason. His two half-brothers, Muhammad and Jarrah, would be sound asleep. Mubarak's middle-of-the-night arrival was sure to take them by surprise.

Muhammad and Jarrah were full brothers in the al-Sabah family, the clan that had ruled Kuwait since the middle of the 18th century. Muhammad al-Sabah was the ruler in name, but Jarrah exercised so much influence and power over his brother that it was as if the two men ruled the country jointly.

Many people living in Kuwait at the time felt that Muhammad was a weak and ineffectual leader who had allowed the powerful Ottoman Turks to gain too much influence over him and the region in general. Mubarak was nearly certain that the Turks, aided by a wealthy Kuwaiti merchant named Yusuf Ibrahim, were poised to take over Kuwait. After nearly 200 years of rule by members of the al-Sabah family, Mubarak was not about to let control of Kuwait slip through his half-brothers' fingers.

Muhammad and Jarrah apparently did not think much of Mubarak. They had recently sent him off to the desert for the ostensible purpose of subduing unruly Bedouin tribes that were forcing their protection upon desert travelers. Not only did this task take him far from the palace, where all the important political decisions were made; Mubarak was given no funds for the assignment. Many later interpreted this as a sign that the two blood brothers had a plot of their own in the works.

Shortly after being exiled to the desert, Mubarak, who was known for his familiarity with the desert peoples and their ways, quickly strengthened his alliances with tribal leaders. Then, when he was confident of their support, Mubarak made his move. The time had come to end his half-brothers' reign.

On the night of May 8, 1896, when Mubarak and his men reached the royal palace, Mubarak himself quickly scaled the palace walls. His half-brother Muhammad was sound asleep on the roof. Mubarak drew his gun and fired one shot. Then, when Muhammad cried out, fearfully pleading for his brother's mercy, Mubarak pointed the gun again. This time the shot was fatal. While Mubarak confronted Muhammad, one of his sons tracked down the other brother, Jarrah, and stabbed him to death.

After the murders, Mubarak forbade the palace servants

to leave, to prevent word of his coup d'etat from spreading. The next morning Kuwaitis gathered at the palace, as was the custom, to seek an audience with the sheik. To their surprise, neither Muhammad nor Jarrah was anywhere to be seen.

Dramatically, Mubarak waited until the room was full. Then he pulled out his sword and lay it across his knee as he proclaimed himself the new sheik of Kuwait. He invited the people present to speak, but no one dared to object to him or his news. Later, when the Kuwaiti people outside the palace walls heard about the extraordinary coup, a crowd came to the palace to pay homage to Mubarak.

Despite the seemingly smooth transition that took place inside the palace, Mubarak's succession was not completely without opposition. Upon learning of the murder of the brothers, Yusuf Ibrahim, the rich merchant who had reportedly been cultivating a relationship with the Turks, quickly began trying to consolidate his own influence in the region. He contacted the Ottoman-controlled governor of nearby Basra, hoping to gain his support, and also banded with some members of the al-Sabah clan that had been close to Muhammad and Jarrah. But Mubarak was an astute politician, too. He in turn traveled to the Ottoman governor of Baghdad, to gain favor there. And he already had the support of the Bedouins, the desert people. In the end, Mubarak's sphere of influence extended further than Ibrahim's. Deftly, he managed to hold onto the power he had seized.

Mubarak's seizure of power by force remains the only violent transfer of power in Kuwait's history. And although Mubarak became the ruler by murdering his half-brothers, he quickly established himself as a dynamic, and even popular, leader who would in time come to be called "Mubarak the Great." Under Sheik Mubarak, Kuwait transformed itself from a loosely defined sheikdom with ties to the Ottoman Empire to an autonomous state that was

The Bedouins supported Mubarak in his overthrow of Muhammad al-Sabah. Bedouins, such as those pictured here in the 1870s, are Arabs who live in tents and travel across the deserts where they search for water and pastures for their livestock.

backed by England. Some Kuwaitis condemned Mubarak's political strategy, charging that the close alliance he deliberately forged with England merely replaced what had been a similar alliance with the Ottoman Turks. But others see Mubarak the Great as the sheik who saved Kuwait from Ottoman domination and the one who paved the way to future wealth by establishing strong ties to England.

No matter how Mubarak's violent coup of 1896 and subsequent reign are interpreted, one thing is undeniable: He entered the political arena at a critical time in Kuwaiti history. Because of his place in time, he was charged with the formidable task of leading a poor, underdeveloped country, whose economy was based on fishing and pearling, into the 20th century. And because of his forceful personality, and his vision of Kuwait's status in the Persian Gulf, he secured his country's independent status. Moreover, the new relationships he cultivated with regions outside the Gulf States had a dramatic impact on the shape that Kuwait's oil industry took once oil was discovered, pointing the way toward unimaginable prosperity, not only for the al-Sabah, but also for the people of their kingdom.

A caravan of camels passes by the city of Aleppo, which lies in the hills of northwestern Syria. Today the city is an important agricultural and industrial center.

# 2

# The al-Sabah Dynasty

K uwait is a small nation, about the size of New Jersey, that sits along the northwestern shore of the Persian Gulf. Iraq borders the country to the north and west. Saudi Arabia lies to the southwest, and across the Persian Gulf is Iran.

Archaeological evidence suggests that few people resided in Kuwait until the early 18th century. The region surrounding it has an ancient history. The Greek conqueror Alexander the Great, who lived from 356 to 323 B.C., dreamed of creating an empire that stretched from Egypt to Persia and India. He set out with his army and began conquering lands. But he died in Babylon at age 33, before accomplishing his goal. The empire he had formed up to that time was divided among his generals. The land that is today known as Kuwait was controlled by the Greeks from the fourth to first centuries B.C.

In 170 A.D., a Roman historian named Arrain wrote about the conquests of Alexander the Great. He described one of Alexander's admirals, a man named Nearchos, sailing along the Indus River and exploring the Arabian coast. It is believed that one island he wrote about was Faylakah—a Kuwaiti island where Greeks lived around 300 B.C. After the Romans defeated the Greeks, few additional mentions of Kuwait are found.

## MUHAMMAD AND THE SPREAD OF ISLAM

The prophet Muhammad was born in Mecca, southwest of Kuwait on the Arabian Peninsula in about 570 A.D. In 610, when he was about 40 years old, he had his first revelation from God. According to Karen Armstrong's *Islam: A Short History,* Muhammad was terrified by the presence "which squeezed him tightly until he heard the first words of a new Arab scripture pouring from his lips." Muhammad did not tell anyone but his wife and her cousin about the revelations. Two years later, in 612, Muhammad finally began preaching about what had been revealed to him.

The prophet taught no new doctrines. Instead he reminded people about the presence of one God rather than the many idols being worshipped at the time. Muhammad also preached about the importance of sharing wealth and treating the sick and poor with kindness and respect.

Over the next 21 years, the *Qu'ran* (or Koran) was revealed to Muhammad verse by verse, sometimes in direct response to issues among his community of followers. These revelations, often recited in public places, won converts because of the beautiful way in which they were expressed. In revealing God's word, Muhammad was simultaneously creating a new form of Arab prose and poetry.

His new sect eventually became known as *Islam*, translated into English as "Submission to God." A person who submitted to God, or Allah, and his doctrine to treat one another with justice and compassion was called a Muslim. Muslims were required to pray three times each day (this later became five times). They also gave a portion of their incomes to the poor and fasted during the holy month of Ramadan.

Muhammad also preached tolerance, insisting that Muslims respect the beliefs of Jews and Christians. He also maintained that he was not completely rejecting tradition; instead, the old religion was not working. Widespread spiritual poverty, warfare, and social injustice were all proof of its inefficacy.

Muhammad gradually gained a small following of about 70 families. At first, he was largely ignored in his hometown of Mecca. However, by 616, the political leaders spoke out against him, angrily charging him with denigrating the faith of their fathers and pretending to be a prophet.

In 622 the Muslim families in Mecca began migrating (*hijrah*), one by one, to Yathrib, where Muhammad had won over monotheistic tribes living there. Yathrib later became known as Medina, and this hijrah marks the beginning of the Muslim era.

Muhammad died in 632. However, through his teachings he left an important legacy. Islam spread rapidly among Arabian tribes, challenging the powerful Ottoman and Persian Empires. A battle between these early followers of Islam and the Persians was fought near the head of the Persian Gulf around 632. Some historians suspect this battle was actually located at Kadhima on the north shore of Kuwait Bay. The Arab soldiers led by Khalid surprisingly defeated the Persians, who had brought along chains for binding their Arab prisoners. This battle became known as "the Battle of the Chains."

Power in the Islamic Empire gradually shifted from

Mecca and Medina in Saudi Arabia, to Syria, and also to Baghdad in Iraq. From 1258 through the 18th century, the Mongols ruled this region, or at least sections of it. The Ottoman Turks gradually began to dominate and held most of the power until the end of World War I, in 1918. However, these empires did not exercise much power in the areas around Kuwait.

Another influence in the Persian Gulf came from Portugal in the 16th century. The great Portuguese sailors traveled to the Arabian Gulf (as the Persian Gulf is called in the region), where they traded goods, battled the Ottomans, and built fortresses. The names of several Kuwaiti places appear on Portuguese maps. As Portuguese seafaring power waned, the British began to dominate the seas.

Before the early 1700s, few people lived in this harsh desert environment. Sometime between 1710 and 1716, a drought struck central Arabia. Bedouin people, known as *Bani Utub* (people who trek or move), were forced to leave central Arabia in search of water and fresh pastures for their animals. Along the southern shore of Kuwait Bay, which feeds into the Persian Gulf, they found the fresh water and foliage they needed. It is unclear exactly when the settlers established a home in what is today known as Kuwait City, but it is generally thought to be around 1716.

## THE AL-SABAH FAMILY

Ancestors of the al-Sabah family, which still rules Kuwait today, were among these early settlers. The group named their new home *Kuwait*, which means "fort," or, more specifically, "little fortress on a hill near the water."

These early residents of Kuwait seemed determined to live peacefully. Although the area had few inhabitants, it was controlled by a powerful tribe of northeast Arabia—the Bani Khalid. The Kuwaitis soon established cooperative relations with the Bani Khalid by marrying women from the tribe.

The early settlers also confronted a threat from the powerful Ottoman Empire, which also claimed Kuwait as its own. The Kuwaitis sent a delegation to the Ottomans at Basra (now part of Iraq) to relay their wish to live peacefully. The chief of this Kuwaiti delegation was the head of the al-Sabah family. He was called the *sheik*, or leader of the tribe. Between 1756 and 1762, the group elected the sheik to rule them as Sabah I. Since this time, the sheik of Kuwait has always been a descendant of the Sabah family.

Not a lot is known about Sabah I. It is believed that he was born around 1674 and his father's name was Jaber. His family probably came to Kuwait in the early part of the 18th century. Under his rule, Kuwaitis took advantage of their location near the water by building up their fleet of ships and developing trade routes. In a 1756 traveler's report it was said about the Kuwaitis:

> They . . . have some three hundred vessels, but almost all are small because they employ them only for pearl diving. This and fishing during the winter is their only occupation. They number about four thousand men armed with swords, shields, and lances.

Markets opened up near the center of town where goods could be bought and traded then sometimes delivered to the Arabian interior. Kuwait became a modest staging post on the trade route from Persia, India, and southern Arabia to Europe. The country was a popular stop because the Kuwaitis were able to provide a safe haven from attacks at sea and warring Arab traders.

After the death of Sabah I in 1756, his youngest son Abdullah took over and ruled until 1814. Under Abdullah I, Kuwait continued to grow and prosper. Kuwaiti profits from trade and shipping were invested in bigger ships. As a result, Kuwait developed into a major center for shipbuilding. The larger vessels were used in transit trade and as warships. The Kuwaitis soon possessed one of the finest fleets in the Persian Gulf.

In 1765 a Danish traveler named Carsten Neibuhr visited Kuwait. According to his record, the Kuwaitis subsisted by fishing and pearl diving. He wrote that they owned more than 800 boats, and on days when the wind was right for sailing, the town almost completely emptied out. During these early years, the settlers' homes were made of mud and faced the sea. They built their shelters close together, forming a close community not unlike a city.

By 1775 the area had also become an important center for British trade. The British East India Company made Kuwait the starting point for its desert mail service to Aleppo, Syria. This route was part of a system that carried goods and mail from India to England. In 14 to 20 days, camel riders could transport mail across the desert. Enormous caravans, sometimes consisting of as many as 5,000 camels and 1,000 men, could deliver goods in about 80 days.

When the Kuwaitis found they needed help defending their land, they looked to the British East India Company. It was the British who provided cannons and men to help fight against the Wahhabis, a tribe from central Arabia that followed a religious leader known as Muhammad bin Abdul Wahhab. The Wahhabis wreaked havoc upon British trade by intercepting the British East India Company's mail and attacking mail carriers. Finally, the British were forced to abandon Kuwait as a trade route.

Another threat came from pirates at sea. Rahma ibn Jaber was a particularly fierce one. His fleet of about six ships allowed him to terrorize shipping traffic in the Persian Gulf. Once again the British intervened by sending ships from their navy.

By the time of Abdullah I's death in 1814, he was

revered and respected. Jaber I succeeded him. He ruled for over 40 years, from 1814 to 1859, and was especially beloved by his subjects. He was called "Jabir Al Aish," or "Jaber of Rice," because of his habit of generously feeding the poor.

Jaber also did his best to stay apart from the conflicts between the Ottomans and Egyptians. His diplomacy won him many allies—and many gifts. He became the first al-Sabah to be considered wealthy.

Jaber I died in 1859 and was succeeded by Sabah II. As ruler, Sabah II maintained Kuwait's policy of nonalignment in foreign affairs, especially protecting Kuwait from an Ottoman takeover. Like Jaber before him, he maintained order between the Egyptians and Ottomans and reaped rewards from European trading companies that traveled through Kuwait. Under Jaber I and Sabah II, the merchants prospered as well.

By the end of the 19th century, however, the influence of the Ottoman Turks over Kuwaiti affairs was growing. Sheik Abdullah II, who ruled from 1866 to 1892, became known as the ruler who aligned Kuwait with the Ottoman Turks. Under Abdullah II, the distance maintained by his predecessors became more difficult because Midhat Pasha, the Turkish governor of Baghdad, had definite ambitions to incorporate eastern Arabia into the Ottoman Empire. Realizing that Pasha's army might present a danger, Abdullah befriended Pasha and allowed him to use Kuwait as a military base. Abdullah also sent a force of cavalry and 300 boats for Pasha's military campaigns. In return, the sheik received material rewards and was named the *qaimaqam*, or commandant, of the local Ottoman administration, a post he accepted.

Abdullah II died in 1892 at age 78. Muhammad I, the second son of Sabah II, was named the new sheik.

Muhammad immediately announced that his adminis-tration would be as pro-Ottoman as Abdullah's had been. He put his brother Jarrah in charge of financial affairs. His half brother Mubarak, known for his adventurous and outspoken ways, kept his title as commander of the armed forces.

Many Kuwaiti notables (influential people) were displeased with the policies of Muhammad I, complaining that he did not consult them. They felt he listened only to Jarrah and Yusuf Ibrahim, a prominent merchant.

Ibrahim's influence particularly bothered people. He owned large estates in Iraq, which was controlled by the Ottomans. His plans for Kuwait seemed to include the "Ottomanization" or "Iraqization" of Kuwait. The notables, along with Mubarak, also feared that Ibrahim was about to seize control of Kuwait for himself. It was in this uncertain atmosphere that people began to turn to Mubarak for his opinion on political matters—and he began to formulate his plan to murder his half-brothers.

## MUBARAK THE GREAT

After the 1896 coup in which Mubarak seized power, he quickly set about strengthening his country's vulnerable position. Mubarak turned once again to the British, appealing to them to sign a defensive treaty with his country. The British were reluctant at first, not wanting to risk alienating the powerful Ottomans. However, the persuasive Mubarak continued to apply pressure, and then fearing that Kuwait might sign a treaty with the Germans instead, Great Britain finally consented. In 1899 a treaty was signed. This document, sometimes referred to as "the Exclusive Agreement," promised that the British would protect Kuwait. In exchange, Great Britain was also guaranteed access to valuable sea-lanes in the Gulf. Kuwait also pledged not to give up territory or meet with foreign officials without Great Britain's consent. In essence Kuwait handed over to England control of foreign affairs.

The agreement was kept secret at first. However, England quickly became embroiled in Kuwaiti conflicts with the Ottomans as well as other Arab rivals. According to *Beyond the Storm: A Gulf Crisis Reader,* England "became increasingly drawn into protecting the sheikdom. The secret treaty soon became a standing obligation."

Made confident by the formal British backing, the ambitious, grand-thinking Mubarak wanted to check the Turks, who still exerted so much control in the Persian Gulf region. The British, however, were less enthusiastic about this plan. Part of their relationship with Kuwait soon involved the management of Mubarak and his grand schemes. In 1904 they sent a political agent to Kuwait whose job it was in part to monitor the sheik and his dealings with other Arab states.

One of Mubarak's most significant political innovations was his centralization of power under the ruler. Before Mubarak, the sheik had been more of a tribal leader—selected in part by notable Kuwaitis and answerable to them as well. Mubarak, however, made nearly all political decisions on his own, beginning with his coup and continuing this trend throughout his reign. His actions alienated many of the leading families of Kuwait, who felt themselves losing some of their former political clout.

In 1905, Mubarak's old rival, the merchant Yusuf Ibrahim, died. This eased tensions between Mubarak and the heirs of Muhammad and Jarrah, allowing for a series of arranged marriages that were designed to reunite the extended al-Sabah family. In the meantime, since 1903 or so, Kuwait had been experiencing a period of rapid commercial growth. This made it possible for Sheik Mubarak to leave the palace more frequently, traveling on his yacht or camping among the desert tribes that had always strongly supported him.

Under Mubarak, Kuwait became in many ways a more

civilized place to live. Kuwait City grew into a popular resort spot for people in the area, despite the intense summer heat. Mubarak also invited missionaries from the Dutch Reformed Church in the United States to set up a medical center. The center administered medical care in Kuwait from 1911 until years later, when the country could afford to build its own hospitals and medical facilities.

A Christian missionary who met Mubarak in 1911 wrote, "Mubarak held the destinies of Kuwait in the hollow of his hand. Of slender build, with thick-set inscrutable eyes that looked through a man with unerring judgment, he had a face that betokened inflexible purpose and towering strength."

World War I broke out in 1914. Kuwait immediately sided with England and the Allies. Mubarak did his best to help England by assisting in the protection of British oil installations and opening the way to the occupation of Basra. In exchange for this Kuwaiti support, the British promised to exempt Mubarak's date gardens, which were in neighboring Iraq, from tax status. They also promised that his title to these valuable, fruit-producing gardens would be protected and that his family would remain as sheiks of Kuwait.

By 1915, Mubarak was often ill. In November of that year he developed malaria, and he died on November 28. His son, Jaber II, became the new ruler.

Many Kuwaitis were glad to see Jaber succeed his father. In his mid-50s, Jaber II was known as an easygoing man, less dogmatic and volatile than Mubarak. However, Jaber ruled Kuwait for only one year and three months. In January 1917, he suffered an attack of acute gastritis, an inflammation of the digestive tract. He died on February 5, 1917. Another son of Mubarak, Salim, became the new sheik.

Peace was established in Europe by 1918. The Ottomans, who had sided with the Germans, lost their empire when World War I ended. The European allies—Russia, France, and Great Britain—broke up Ottoman territories with a series of agreements that created a number of future border disputes.

Meanwhile, trouble had been brewing in Saudi Arabia, Kuwait's neighbor to the southwest. Years earlier, Mubarak had provided protection to an important Saudi ruling tribe, the Saud, when they were pushed out by enemies. When the Saud were later restored as rulers of Saudi Arabia, relations between the two countries were relatively stable and strong. Sheik Salim, however, sparked Saudi anger when he sheltered members of an enemy tribe. When Salim succeeded Jaber II in 1917, the Saud remembered Salim's support of an enemy and attacked Kuwait. As a result, tensions between Kuwait and Saudi Arabia remained high until Sheik Salim's death in 1921.

## THE CONFERENCE OF UQAIR

An important issue for the sheiks in the early part of the 20th century was the constant dispute of boundaries in the region by countries across the Arabian Peninsula. The Saudis claimed all of Kuwait, while Iraq claimed much of the same land. Meanwhile, the Wahhabis, the tribe from central Arabia, were trying to expand their power by launching another round of attacks. Finally, in November 1922, the Conference of Uqair was held to resolve some of these territorial disputes.

The British presided at this meeting, which was held in Uqair, a port in eastern Arabia. The Saudi ruler Abdul Aziz ibn Saud was there, along with Sabih Beg, the Iraqi minister of communication and works. Major J.C. More, the political agent in Kuwait at the time, attended the conference to represent the sheik of Kuwait. Sir Percy Cox, who was serving as British high commissioner in Iraq, used what has

Oil refineries are part of the landscape in Kuwait. The first barrel of Kuwaiti oil was exported to Great Britain in 1946.

# 3
# The Drilling Begins

## KUWAIT OIL COMPANY, LTD.

When Sheik Salim died in 1921, the al-Sabah family faced no serious threats to their rule. However, Sheik Salim's death brought to light an underlying tension between the ruling al-Sabahs and the merchants that made up a large sector of Kuwaiti society. In recent years these merchants had been clamoring for a bigger say in governing the country.

When Salim died, the merchants formed a council for the purpose of demanding a voice in the government. They especially wanted to have a say in naming Sheik Salim's successor. The council drafted a list of three members of the al-Sabah family. From this list, the al-Sabahs eventually chose Ahmad Jaber al-Sabah.

The council of merchants certainly did not represent a radical transformation of Kuwaiti government. However, the meeting was important in paving the way for reforms that would come later. (It especially helped to set the stage for the creation of the Majlis al-Umma, the Legislative Assembly, in 1938.)

The early part of Sheik Ahmad I's rule was marked by financial instability around the world. A blockade of trade by the Saudis in 1929 caused financial hardship for Kuwaiti merchants who were dependent upon the Saudis for trade. In the United States, the Great Depression struck, sending financial ripples around the world. In the 1930s the Japanese introduced cultured pearls, which could be produced under artificial conditions. This drove down the price of pearls and was disastrous for the Kuwaiti economy. This was a serious blow to Kuwaiti merchants, many of whom had made their living from the pearl market for years. In 1914 there were about 500 pearling boats working in Kuwait; by 1945 only 5 boats remained.

In the meantime, bands of Saudi tribesmen, unwilling or unable to observe the new boundaries put in place at the Conference of Uqair, continued to raid the country and cross into Kuwaiti territory to graze their livestock. Sheik Ahmad finally responded to their raids by commandeering all the automobiles available in Kuwait at the time. Using just 15 cars, Kuwaiti soldiers were able to put a stop to the raiders. This became the first desert battle in which motor vehicles were used.

The most pressing issue of the day was what to do about oil. For a long time it had been believed that huge oil reserves were available in the Middle East. Drilling had begun in nearby countries, and prospectors were looking into the possibility of oil existing in Kuwait as well. However, locating oil is not as easy as it might seem.

Most geologists believe that petroleum, or oil, has formed from the remains of organisms that died millions of years ago. These remains drifted to the ocean floor, where they became trapped in sediments. The sediments gradually built up and then sunk below the ocean floor. There, they were compressed in sedimentary rock that underwent a series of chemical changes that sometimes resulted in the formation of oil. Over time the oil moves upward through cracks and crevices in the rock.

Before 1900 the only way to prospect for oil was to search for oil seepage with very rudimentary equipment, such as a pick, a shovel, and maybe even a divining rod. After 1900, more scientific tools for oil exploration were developed, such as the gravimeter, which measures the pull of gravity at the earth's surface; the magnetometer, which records changes in the earth's magnetic field; and the seismograph, which measures the speed of sound waves traveling beneath the earth's surface. However, even with more precise data and sophisticated tools, drilling remained a risk. Even today, less than a 10 percent chance exists that oil will actually be found at the drilling site.

In the early part of the 20th century, when prospectors' findings seemed to point to the presence of oil in Kuwait, Sheik Ahmad confronted a decision of enormous importance: whether to let foreign oil companies drill for oil. An influential British political officer at the time, Lieutenant Colonel H.R.P. Dickson, told the sheik that if oil were found, Kuwait could become very wealthy. However, Colonel Dickson also warned that the growth of an oil industry would bring sweeping changes to Kuwaiti society, some impossible to foresee.

But Sheik Ahmad eventually decided to give the go-ahead. According to Leila Merrel Foster's *Kuwait*, Sheik Ahmad said, "I must do this for my people, even if it will bring undesirable things to my country. We are poor, pearling is not what it used to be, so I must sign."

In 1934, Sheik Ahmad granted a joint concession to Gulf Oil of the United States and Anglo Persian Oil of Great Britain. The two companies formed the Kuwait Oil Company, Ltd., and in 1936, deep drilling began. Sure enough, under the desert at Burgan, vast quantities of oil were found. This area was destined to become one of the largest and most productive oil fields in the world. So began the dramatic transition of Kuwait's economy from one based mostly on fishing and pearl diving to one based almost completely on oil.

## THE MAJLIS MOVEMENT

In the late 1930s, Kuwaiti merchants began demanding governmental reforms again. The push for reform was fueled in part by King Ghazi in Iraq, who pronounced the emir as the leader of an archaic monarchy. His words struck a chord. And while the merchants had managed to hold on to their political clout because of their importance to the Kuwaiti economy, the discovery of oil reserves became a new threat to their power.

In 1938 a group of prominent Kuwaiti merchants met to discuss their situation and demand more public services from the government. However, the government managed to disrupt the meeting. Not to be deterred, the

Drilling for oil in Kuwait began in the 1930s. Derricks, such as this one used by Britain's Anglo Persian Oil Company, were used for drilling under the desert.

merchants convened again. At this second convocation, they elected a Legislative Assembly, called the *Majlis al-Umma,* which was composed of 14 members.

Under pressure for reform, Sheik Ahmad briefly permitted the assembly to function. However, six months later, fearing that the merchants might be gaining support from officials in Iraq, Ahmad invented a pretext to dissolve the assembly.

The legislative body established in 1938 did not become a permanent fixture of Kuwait's government at this time. Yet this drive for reform, known as the Majlis Movement, influenced future reforms. In fact, the merchant opposition organized itself at a key moment in history—on the eve of Kuwait's emergence as a major exporter of oil to the West. This kept the al-Sabahs keenly aware of the merchants' potential as a political influence while the al-Sabahs were making important decisions regarding the oil industry. The Majlis Movement also played a role in how the al-Sabahs decided to distribute the country's wealth later on, when oil began bringing the country billions of dollars in annual revenue.

One year later, in 1939, World War II broke out in Europe. Because of the war and disruption to labor and transportation, the rich new oil wells had to be plugged. Drilling was ceased until after the war. When the drilling resumed in 1945, more deposits of oil were found at Wafra, North Fawaris, Umm Qadeer, Al Manageesh, Mutriba, and Rawdatain. Additional deposits were found offshore. The Kuwaitis installed more pipelines and building facilities to support their burgeoning oil industry.

In June 1946 the first barrel of oil was exported from Kuwait. Sheik Ahmad was present for this historic occasion. He turned the silver valve wheel on a pipe, loading the first Britain-bound tanker with oil. With this ceremonious gesture, the Sheik also opened wide his country's door to unimaginable wealth.

Sheik Abdullah III guided his country through great changes. Under his rule Kuwait became independent from Great Britain and joined the United Nations, OPEC, and the Arab League. He ruled for 15 years, until his death in 1965.

# 4

# Prosperity

ith oil rapidly flowing to other countries around the world, Kuwaitis wanted to have more control over their expanding oil business. However, most of the policy and management decisions were still being made by the British and American owners of the Kuwait Oil Company.

In 1950, Sheik Ahmad I died at age 65. His successor was Sheik Abdullah III. Many Kuwaitis consider Abdullah III the greatest of their modern rulers. Calm and frugal, he was also revered for his emphasis on tolerance and fair play. Under a 1951 agreement, the sheik shared 50 percent of the profits of the Kuwait Oil Company. With revenue pouring into the country as rapidly as oil flowed out of it, Sheik Abdullah III decided to expand the country's educational and public works programs.

One of the most important issues facing the new sheik was creating a labor pool big enough to meet the rapidly expanding economy. Most Kuwaiti citizens were completely unprepared to deal with the dramatic changes taking place in their country. Oil profits created new opportunities for jobs in real estate, construction, services, and other industries. But because of the lack of training of its own people and the pressure to fill jobs quickly, the government had little choice but to contract out for European, Arab, and Asian workers. This meant a rapid influx of immigrants.

To offset the changes in the population, the Kuwaiti government began to hand out greater privileges to Kuwaiti nationals, who had in fact become a minority in their own country. In December 1959, the Naturalization Decree was instituted. This restricted Kuwaiti citizenship to those residents that had lived in the state since 1920. It also retained the right to vote as a privilege for male Kuwaiti nationals only. Additional regulations prevented foreigners from holding civil positions or purchasing land.

## KUWAITI INDEPENDENCE

In the meantime, British interests in the Persian Gulf and at home had gradually changed. The relationship between Kuwait and Great Britain was beginning to seem outdated. England had already transferred control of Kuwait's postal services and health services. Sir Gawain Bell, the political agent in Kuwait from 1955 to 1957, began to press the sheik for reform—especially the establishment of a representative government. In neighboring Iraq, the monarchs King Faisal and Prince Abdul Ilah were killed and replaced with a republic consisting of a three-man Sovereignty Council and a premier, or prime minister, named General Abdul-Karim

However, as soon as the UN force evacuated, President Nasser of Egypt sent in large numbers of Egyptian troops. The Israelis, afraid of an attack by Egypt, launched a surprise air strike. Several of Kuwait's neighbors—Syria, Jordan, and Iraq—joined in the ensuing battle.

When this war between the Arabs and Israel broke out in 1967, Kuwait joined with other Arab nations in an oil embargo against the United States and the United Kingdom, both of which sided with Israel. In the United States the embargo created high gasoline prices and long lines at filling stations. Kuwait further supported the Arab world by providing monetary aid to Egypt and Jordan along with an army of Palestinian guerrilla fighters because of its large Palestinian population. The UN ended the war with a cease-fire the next week, but this conflict, known as the Six-Day War, had the lasting effect of sharpening divisions between Arabs and Jews living in the Middle East.

While Kuwaiti citizens were enjoying the country's prosperity, dissatisfaction with the system of monarchy continued to plague the al-Sabahs. Many people felt that public officials were corrupt and ineffective. Moreover, they believed that the royal family exerted too much control over the press and the legislature. In 1973 the al-Sabah family approved an election to the legislature, called the National Assembly, and a committee was formed to review the constitution.

In 1973, Iraq again threatened to invade Kuwait. Iraqi troops occupied a Kuwaiti border outpost at Samtah. The troops were quickly evacuated, but the Iraqis were demanding access to two Kuwaiti islands: Bubiyan and Warbah, which overlooked an Iraqi port. If Iraq could control them, or at least have access, the country would obtain its goal of gaining a deeper seaport in the Persian Gulf. Kuwait, however, refused to make any kind of agreement regarding the islands. In response to this new Iraqi threat, the country also began expanding its armed forces, creating a navy, and adopting a policy of compulsory military service for its citizens.

In October 1973, another Arab–Israeli war erupted. This conflict was named the Yom Kippur War because Egyptian and Syrian forces attacked Israeli positions along the Suez Canal and in the Golan Heights on Yom Kippur, the most sacred Jewish holy day. Kuwait again demonstrated its loyalty to the Arab world by sending troops and giving financial aid. It also used its vast oil supplies to try to influence the West to end its support of Israel. By limiting oil exports to the United States and Great Britain, Kuwait hoped to force Israel to withdraw from occupied Arab territory.

Between the years 1974 and 1984, manufacturing grew in Kuwait at a rate of about 6.5 percent. In 1976 the government nationalized the Kuwait Oil Company, which had been owned by British Petroleum and Gulf Oil. The following year, Kuwait took over control of onshore production in the Divided Zone between Kuwait and Saudi Arabia. At the same time, the government was facing the fact that the nation's oil reserves were not going to last forever. A conscious decision was made to diversify the types of industry in Kuwait.

New industrial zones were established at Shuaib, Shuwaikh, and Ahmadi. The new industrial development included fertilizer, salt, and chlorine factories. However, expansion was monitored closely because of concerns about the need for foreign labor. The government did not want to risk another dramatic spike in immigration. Animal husbandry, fishing, construction, and the service industry were other areas of diversification.

In 1976, protesting the practice of the members of the National Assembly to criticize the cabinet and its policies, the cabinet resigned. Members of the cabinet claimed that the assembly made day-to-day governing of the country exceedingly difficult. Concerned by the number of disagreements, and the ties between the Kuwaiti opposition and factions in the Arab world, the emir suspended the constitution and dissolved the assembly. He asked the crown prince to form a new cabinet, but elections for a new assembly were not held again until 1981.

On December 31, 1977, Sheik Sabah III died of cancer at age 52. The Crown Prince Sheik Jaber III succeeded him, and Sheik Saad was named the new crown prince. These two al-Sabah men still hold these titles today.

The new emir, Jaber III, was born in 1926. Like Sabah III before him, he had served in high-ranking government positions, including head of public security, head of the Department of Finance, and director of Kuwait's oil policy. When Sabah III became emir in 1965, Jaber was appointed prime minister, and in 1966 he was endorsed as the crown prince.

The new crown prince, Saad al-Sabah, began his career in Kuwait's Metropolitan Police, serving as its deputy head under his uncle, Sheik Sabah III. He later served as minister of the interior and minister of defense. He was endorsed as heir apparent on January 31, 1978, and named prime minister on February 8, 1978.

## THE IRAN-IRAQ WAR

Jaber III faced his first major crisis as emir in January 1979, when the Shah of Iran was toppled from power. Ruhollah Khomeini became the new leader of the Islamic Republic of Iran. Khomeini was a Shiite, a religious fundamentalist who called for an Islamic Revolution.

Shah Pahlavi of Iran, shown here with his wife, Farah, was deposed and forced to flee his country in January 1979. The new Iranian leader, Ayatollah Khomeini, retaliated against Kuwait for its support of Iraq during the Iran–Iraq conflicts in the 1980s.

While Shiite Muslims were a minority group in Kuwait, they formed the majority in Iran. The Shiites had broken away from other Muslims shortly after the prophet Muhammad's death. They believed that Ali, the prophet's son-in-law, and his descendants should be chosen as leaders of the faith, a doctrine known as legitimism. Shiites also followed the basic five pillars of Islam; however, they differed on the interpretation of certain Islamic teachings and had developed their own calendar.

The new Iranian ruler, known as the *ayatollah*, which means "sign of God," immediately began putting strict

Islamic laws in place in Iran, severely restricting the activities of its citizens. The Ayatollah also began attempting to spread his revolution to other Muslim countries in the Middle East. Many of his followers used terrorist acts, such as suicide bombings, and plane hijackings, to carry out their mission.

The situation became even more dangerous in September of the following year, 1980, when Iraq invaded Iran. Iraq's invasion of Iran was the result of boundary disputes, as well as of internal rebellions from the Kurds who lived in the north of Iraq, and Shiite Muslims, who lived in the south. Both of these groups supported Iran, angering Iraq. Saddam Hussein, the president of Iraq, believed that the Ayatollah's 1979 revolution had weakened Iran. It was an opportune time for him to increase his own country's power in the region.

Kuwait promptly threw its support to Iraq and to Saddam Hussein, donating billions of dollars to Hussein's war effort and appealing to the West on his behalf. Iran retaliated for this show of support. Oil installations and tankers in Kuwait were bombed by Shiite Muslims associated with Iran. There was also a dramatic attempt to assassinate the emir by driving a car loaded with a bomb into a procession of cars. As a result of these acts, many Iranians were deported from Kuwait.

In 1986 and 1987, Iran also seized Kuwaiti merchant ships, stealing their cargo. To protect its oil fleet, Kuwait began registering these ships as American, British, Russian, or Liberian. Many countries lent minesweeping operations to assist Kuwait with its defense while Iran continued these assaults.

In 1985 and 1986, the members of the National Assembly pressed for greater access to the policy-making process. Members also criticized the government's recent mishandling of a crisis involving the Souk-al-Manakh, Kuwait's stock market. Moreover, as the war against Iran continued, sessions of the assembly were filled with long tirades against Iran. To the emir, who feared an attack from Iran, democracy suddenly seemed like a luxury that his nation could not afford.

The emir finally dissolved the National Assembly on July 3, 1986. The principal reason he gave was security concerns related to the Iran–Iraq War. Press censorship began, as did the expulsion of certain editors and journalists. According to official police reports, about 27,000 journalists were deported from Kuwait in 1986.

An article in the constitution granted the emir the power to dissolve the National Assembly, but there was also a clause that stated the Assembly would be reconvened in two months. The 1985 National Assembly was never reconvened. However, Kuwaiti citizens did not immediately demand new elections, at least not until 1990.

In August 1988, after eight years of fighting and extensive damage in both countries, the Iran–Iraq War came to an end. The once powerful Iranian army had been greatly weakened, and Iraq, while largely perceived as the victor, had also suffered extensive damage. Bombs had destroyed oil facilities in southern Iraq, and trade had been a severely disrupted—major blows to the country's economy.

In Kuwait, the end of the war marked a time of cautious optimism about life in the Persian Gulf. Many Kuwaitis assumed war was behind them, despite continued tensions between the Israelis and Palestinians. And natural-born Kuwaitis continued to enjoy prosperity, even sumptuous wealth, with access to free education, free health care, inexpensive housing, and well-paid civil service jobs with generous perks.

There was also the sense that more democratic reforms were about to take place inside. The emir, instead of reconvening the National Assembly, formed a National Council.

This was a partially elected body that had no fiscal or legislative powers. Many Kuwaitis protested the move by boycotting the election. Pro-democracy rallies occurred in the streets, and reform was a constant topic of talk in the *diwaniyas*, informal social gatherings where Kuwaitis frequently discussed politics over tea or strong coffee.

In 1990 many Kuwaitis also assumed that their country's loyal support of Iraq in the war against Iran had won them a valuable ally in President Saddam Hussein. After all, they had loaned Iraq $17 billion and risked Iran's wrath by siding with Iraq. However, Hussein had other intentions when it came it came to Kuwait. These were born out of both a long history of boundary disputes and his country's desperate economic situation after the war. In the summer of 1990, Hussein's agenda became shockingly clear. He was waging a new war—this one against Kuwait.

An Iraqi soldier in Baghdad explains to militia recruits how to use a machine gun. Saddam Hussein used extensive military force in his invasion of Kuwait.

# 5

# Invasion
# of Kuwait

Although Kuwait had supported Iraq in the Iran–Iraq War from 1980 to 1988, Saddam Hussein had been harboring a growing number of grievances against the country. These included conflicts over territory that had been going on for years, over what he claimed was Kuwaiti overproduction of oil, and over Kuwait's refusal to forgive Iraq's sizable war debt.

During the Iran–Iraq War, Iraq had again approached Kuwait about access to the Bubiyan and Warban Islands. Access to these islands would have helped Iraq strategically in the war against Iran. However, Kuwait had refused the request and then did so again in 1989, after the war, further angering the Iraqis. This refusal compounded bitter feelings left over from the 1922 Conference of

Uqair, where Sir Percy Cox had drawn the new borders of Kuwait, Iraq, and Saudi Arabia, leaving Iraq only 36 miles of coastline, compared to Kuwait's 310 miles.

In addition, the Iraqi president believed that Kuwait had been slant-drilling at the Rumaila oilfield—a 50-mile-long, banana-shaped oilfield along Kuwait's border with Iraq. Ninety percent of the oilfield lay in Iraq; and Saddam Hussein charged that Kuwait had pumped over $10 billion of oil that rightfully belonged to Iraq.

Meanwhile, the Iran–Iraq War had cost Iraq an estimated $500 billion, leaving its economy badly crippled. Iraq owed money to Europe, Japan, and the United States, as well as to Saudi Arabia, Kuwait, and the United Arab Emirates. Reconstruction costs, plus these substantial war debts, meant that it would take at least 20 years for Iraq's economy to recover.

When his country entered the war against Iran in 1980, Hussein viewed this not so much as a personal issue or a specifically Iraqi cause, but an Arab cause that he had fought on behalf of all Arab nations. Having done that, he expected Arabs around the world to be grateful to him for halting the Ayatollah's Islamic revolution. And the way for these Arab countries to show their gratitude, he believed, was to forgive the war debts that Iraq had accrued. When Kuwait refused to do so, Hussein considered this to be the equivalent of declaring war upon his country.

Hussein also charged that Kuwait was waging economic war by overproducing oil. At the end of the Baghdad Arab summit in May 1990, Hussein publicly accused Kuwait of deliberately overproducing oil, which drove down the price of crude oil. It also violated OPEC production quotas. According to Hussein, every $1 drop in the price of a barrel of oil meant a loss of $1 billion a year for Iraq.

In addition, Hussein faced mounting pressures at home.

He had stayed in power in Iraq since 1979 largely due to the government's generous provision of goods and services. When the war with Iran ended, Iraqi citizens expected a resumption of many of the things they had enjoyed before. But with the national coffers drained, there was no way to meet the Iraqi people's expectations.

Many historians also believe that Hussein's personality played a role in what unfolded in the Persian Gulf that summer. He had always seen himself as destined to be a great figure in history, specifically as the one supreme leader of the Arab world. This allowed him to justify many of the actions that he was to take regarding Kuwait. And Hussein was intensely proud of his powerful army. When the war with the Iranians was over, he aimed his mighty military machine at the Kurds, the rebellious people in the north. Hussein's troops razed entire villages and released a deadly, poisonous gas—killing at least 5,000 Kurds. Having had so much success with his military brawn, Hussein was confident that he could now seize control of Kuwait with ease.

By June 1990 it was clear that Hussein's hostility toward Kuwait was mounting. He had begun by making the accusations about slant-drilling at Rumaila and overproduction of oil. Next, he began mobilizing Iraqi troops along the Kuwaiti border. By July 23, U.S. intelligence sources reported that at least 30,000 troops were posted there.

Kuwait was not the only country alarmed by Hussein's escalating hostility. Arab leaders from Syria, Jordan, and Saudi Arabia tried to negotiate a solution between the two countries. Diplomats from around the world flew to Iraq to meet with Hussein, pleading with him to avoid war. The Iraqi leader did not move his troops from their position along the border with Kuwait, but he did provide repeated assurances that he was not going to attack. For a few more weeks, this gave the Kuwaitis reason to cling to hope that a peaceful solution might somehow be brokered.

King Fahd of Saudi Arabia was one of the leaders from the Middle East who tried to mediate between Iraq and Kuwait. A meeting in his country failed to bring about a peaceful solution to the crisis.

In late July 1990, King Fahd of Saudi Arabia arranged for a special meeting in Jiddah, Saudi Arabia, to try to settle the dispute peacefully. However, the Iraqis continued making demands upon Kuwait at the meeting, insisting that Kuwait forgive the $17 billion war debt and that the two countries make an agreement regarding the two

Kuwaiti islands, Bubiyan and Warbah. When the Kuwaitis refused to comply, offering to forgive only a small sum instead, the Iraqis walked out of the meeting. The talks had lasted just two hours. Still, most people in the Middle East as well as in the West thought Saddam Hussein was bluffing about his threats to invade Kuwait. They did not believe he would actually follow through.

However, by the time the meeting in Jiddah ended, Kuwait's fate was sealed. At 2:00 A.M. on August 2, 1990, Hussein gave the order. Then the Iraqi army crossed the border into Kuwait, startling both Kuwait and the rest of the world.

Jaber III became emir of Kuwait in 1977 and still serves as ruler. During the Persian Gulf War he ran his government from a safe position in Saudi Arabia.

# 6

# The Persian Gulf War

AUGUST 2, 1990

W hen Iraq invaded Kuwait on the morning of August 2, Emir Jaber III and Crown Prince Saad, along with other members of the family and the cabinet, narrowly escaped by helicopter. They departed just minutes before an attack on the compound by Iraqi helicopters and ground troops began. They landed in Ad Dammam, Saudi Arabia, where they quickly set up an emergency government in exile.

The emir's brother Fahd al-Sabah stayed behind to help defend the palace. In the fighting that broke out there, Fahd was killed, along with about 300 Kuwaiti troops at the Ministry of Defense. When many of the Kuwaiti soldiers realized they were hopelessly outnumbered, they surrendered—only to be brutally slaughtered by the Iraqi forces. That day many residents of Kuwait awoke to the sound of planes flying over the al-Sabah compound and dropping bombs on the buildings. Soon the palace and many other buildings lay in ruins.

By early that day it was clear that the Kuwaiti army was no match for the massive Iraqi forces. Saddam Hussein had sent 100,000 troops, whereas Kuwait's total military strength was only 20,000. Hundreds of Iraqi tanks rolled across the tiny country, and Iraqi jet fighters and attack aircraft filled the sky. Their first targets in Kuwait City were the emir's palace, the central bank where Kuwait's gold reserves were stored, and the Ministry of Information, where radio and television broadcasts were carried out. Within just seven hours, Iraq's Republican Guard and about 350 tanks occupied Kuwait City. Baghdad radio began triumphantly declaring that Iraq had liberated Kuwait from the al-Sabah family on behalf of Kuwaiti revolutionaries who had set up a "Provisional Free Kuwait Government."

The invading Iraqi soldiers quickly confiscated homes, money, cars, and food. Within 24 hours, Iraq had complete control of the whole country. That goal accomplished, thousands of troops then moved to Kuwait's border with Saudi Arabia. To the rest of the world, which was nervously watching these Iraqi maneuvers, it appeared that Iraq was poised to invade Saudi Arabia next.

## RESISTANCE

The invasion had come as such a surprise that the small Kuwaiti army was quickly overcome. Still, many Kuwaiti citizens, organized largely through social institutions such as mosques and cooperative societies, tried to resist the invaders. At night people climbed to the tops

Kuwait's soldiers were no match for the Iraqi troops and weapons. Other nations gathered together and sent forces and equipment to the Persian Gulf in preparation for war against Iraq.

of tall buildings to raise large banners demanding an immediate Iraqi withdrawal. But as more of Hussein's troops arrived, the use of brutal tactics increased. And then when phone lines and broadcast networks were destroyed, organized efforts such as this became more difficult to carry out—and more dangerous as well.

An anti-Iraqi guerrilla movement also formed. These fighters tried to defend their country with guns, grenades, explosives, and even some missiles. But in the end their numbers were too small to have any lasting effect. If anything, the guerrillas' efforts may have increased Iraqi violence toward Kuwaitis.

When a group of children and women marched in Kuwait City to protest the occupation, they were cold-bloodedly shot. Many citizens were brought in for grueling "interrogations," then brought home, only to be shot and killed in front of their families. Women were rounded up and frequently raped and even mutilated. Soon Kuwaitis were required to become Iraqi citizens to be able to get medical care and automobile licenses, or to purchase gasoline and other goods. According to U.S. intelligence officials, the violence against Kuwaitis reflected traditional Arab secret-police tactics. Beatings and rapes were frequent.

## WORLD REACTION

The rest of the world did not wait long to react despite Saddam Hussein's threat to turn Kuwait into a "graveyard" if any outside powers intervened. The United States, Britain, and France jointly condemned the invasion, then froze Iraqi and Kuwaiti assets, banned Iraqi trade, and halted all arms deliveries. The Soviet Union, which was the major supplier of arms to Iraq at the time, suspended military shipments to Iraq. The 12-member European Community condemned Iraq, too, imposing broad sanctions. Together Iraq and Kuwait controlled about 20 percent of the world's oil reserves. In response to the Iraqi occupation, the price of crude oil immediately shot up by 15 percent. In Japan the Nikkei Stock Market fell 593 points.

On August 2 the UN Security Council passed Resolution 660, condemning Iraq's invasion and demanding its withdrawal. The vote was fourteen to zero, with Yemen abstaining.

The Arab world reacted predictably with more caution.

Kuwaiti officials tried to get the Arab League Council, which was meeting in Cairo at the time, to organize a joint force to fight the Iraqi invasion and condemn the action. However, the meeting broke up without such condemnations, perhaps to discourage intervention by outside countries and allow time for a diplomatic solution.

To this end, King Hussein of Jordan tried to organize a mini-summit meeting in Jiddah, Saudi Arabia. He hoped that terms of an Iraqi withdrawal could be hammered out there, optimistically telling U.S. President George Bush that he was working on an Arab solution.

The next day King Hussein met with Saddam Hussein to discuss a plan for an Iraqi withdrawal. But later that day King Hussein's efforts fell apart. Under heavy pressure from Egypt, Britain, and the United States, 13 of 21 Arab League ministers agreed to send military forces to Saudi Arabia and to other Gulf States. Jordan, Sudan, Yemen, Mauritania, and the Palestine Liberation Organization (PLO) abstained from this vote. But 12 member countries endorsed a resolution that condemned Iraq's invasion as well as the military buildup on the border with Saudi Arabia, and demanded the emir's return. King Hussein later said that he had felt betrayed by the United States and others; he had believed he was on the brink of arranging an expedient withdrawal of Iraqi troops.

Meanwhile, world leaders, such as America's President Bush and Britain's Prime Minister Margaret Thatcher, began forming a coalition against Iraq. The members included Afghanistan, Argentina, Australia, Bangladesh, Belgium, Canada, the Czech Republic, Denmark, France, Germany, Greece, Honduras, Hungary, Italy, the Netherlands, New Zealand, Niger, Norway, Pakistan, Poland, Portugal, Senegal, Sierra Leone, Singapore, South Korea, Spain, Sweden, Turkey, the United Kingdom, and the United States. Arab members were Bahrain, Egypt,

Kuwait, Morocco, Oman, Qatar, Saudi Arabia, Syria, and the United Arab Emirates. South Korea was the only coalition member that was not also a member of the UN. The Arab countries of Jordan, Libya, and Yemen opposed the involvement of non-Arab countries but did not fight against the coalition. China and the Soviet Union, the world's most powerful communist countries at the time, did not join the coalition. However, they cooperated as members of the UN Security Council, which allowed the UN to play a large role in the conflict. This coalition of nations worked together to create a "Desert Shield" designed to stop Iraq from invading other Gulf States.

On August 6, under pressure from the United States, the UN Security Council passed Resolution 661, which imposed an embargo, prohibiting all trade with Iraq except for medical supplies and food in certain circumstances. Almost all of Iraq's major trading partners supported this embargo, effectively ending Iraq's foreign trade. The next day, Saudi Arabia invited other nations to send troops to their country to help defend the region. The United States, along with Britain, Canada, France, Australia, and others, sent equipment as well as troops.

Iraq fought back by announcing the permanent annexation of Kuwait as Iraq's 19th province. It disbanded the provisional Kuwaiti government it had established and ordered foreign embassies in Kuwait to close. In response, the UN adopted a resolution declaring the annexation of Kuwait "void."

On August 25 the UN Security Council authorized the use of force to carry out the embargo against Iraq. On November 29 the council adopted Resolution 678, granting permission to use all necessary means to expel Iraq from Kuwait if Iraq did not withdraw by January 15, 1991. The "line in the sand" had been drawn: Iraq had six weeks to remove its troops.

President George Bush, flanked by Defense Secretary Dick Cheney (left) and Chairman of the Joint Chiefs of Staff General Colin Powell, held a press conference at his summer home to discuss the Persian Gulf War.

## THE AIR WAR BEGINS

Meanwhile, the coalition, under U.S. leadership, began building up its military presence in the Persian Gulf. By the middle of January, about 670,000 troops, 3,500 tanks, and 1,800 combat aircraft were stationed there. Iraq had 350,000 to 500,000 troops in Kuwait and southern Iraq, along with 4,500 tanks, 550 combat aircraft, and a small navy.

Despite the coalition's military buildup and the looming deadline, Saddam Hussein did not move his troops. On January 12 the U.S. Congress, both the Senate and the House of Representatives, voted in favor of employing American military force to help liberate Kuwait. When January 15 came and went, Operation Desert Shield officially became Operation Desert Storm.

The air war, led by the United States, began at 3 A.M. on January 17, 1991.

The coalition's initial strategy was to try to force Iraq to withdraw from Kuwait by bombing Iraqi military and industrial targets. Their goals were clear and direct: destroy Iraq's ability to launch attacks, along with the facilities where it was suspected that biological, chemical, and nuclear weapons were being produced. The allies also aimed their attacks on diminishing the Iraqi air force and disrupting their communications networks so that Iraqi troops could not gather information about the coalition's movements or communicate with one another.

Allied aircraft bombed Baghdad, the Iraqi capital, and then attacked locations across Iraq and Kuwait, aiming the bombs at Iraqi troops and tanks, transportation routes, and supplies. New and sophisticated high-tech weapons such as night-vision systems and precision guided weapons were used in combat for the first time—with great success.

Iraq retaliated with weapons of its own. At the start of the air war, Scud missiles were launched at densely popu-lated areas in Saudi Arabia and Israel. Compared to the sophisticated weapons in the coalition's arsenal, the Scuds were inaccurate and primitive, but they met the immediate Iraqi objective—killing and terrifying a number of people in both countries.

By attacking Israel, Saddam Hussein was also trying to lure the Jewish state into the conflict. This way he thought he could present the war as an Arab–Israeli dispute and perhaps threaten the unity of the coalition, which many Arab nations had joined. However, under intense pressure from Western countries, Israel resisted the bait and did not enter the war.

The first major ground battle broke out at Khafji, a small Saudi Arabian town near Kuwait. On January 29,

Iraqi troops occupied Khafji. By January 31, Saudi and Qatari troops, with some U.S. help, recaptured the town.

## THE LIBERATION OF KUWAIT

Despite five weeks of heavy bombing by the coalition, Iraqi troops remained in Kuwait. Diplomatic efforts went on, but disagreements about the specific terms of an Iraqi withdrawal continued. On February 22, President Bush issued an ultimatum: Iraq had 24 hours to accept UN conditions for total evacuation or the United States would launch another assault.

This next deadline expired. The coalition, led in the United States by General H. Norman Schwarzkopf, then launched a major ground attack. On February 24, at 4 A.M., several large military operations occurred at once. U.S. and French troops invaded Iraq from Saudi Arabia, heading swiftly north into Iraq and toward the Euphrates River to cut off Iraqi supply lines and prevent a retreat by the Iraqis. U.S. and British troops also crossed into Iraq from Saudi Arabia. They moved north into Iraq, then headed east to attack Iraqi troops.

Still more coalition forces, made up of U.S. Marines and troops from Kuwait, Egypt, Saudi Arabia, and Syria, attacked Iraqi troops across southern Kuwait. These troops rapidly destroyed Iraqi fortifications and surrounded Iraqi forces, bringing about the surrender of over 60,000 soldiers.

Finally, on February 26, Saddam Hussein ordered his army to leave Kuwait. On February 27 in the United States, President Bush went on television to announce a cease-fire.

"Kuwait is liberated," he declared. "Iraq's army is defeated. Our military objectives are met." The allies were ceasing their military operations, effective at midnight. Only 100 hours after the ground war had begun, Kuwait was officially liberated.

Residents surround an American Special Forces soldier as the news spreads that Kuwait has been liberated from Iraqi forces.

# 7
# Rebuilding Begins

## DAMAGE AND DEVASTATION

When the seven-month occupation by Iraq ended, the Kuwaitis were jubilant. The streets filled with Kuwaiti citizens joyfully celebrating the liberation of their country. People danced in the streets, firing off shots from guns, triumphantly waving American and Kuwaiti flags, and hugging one another in profound relief.

At the start of the war, nearly two-thirds of Kuwaiti citizens had left the country, fleeing to Jordan and Egypt. Eight out of ten foreigners living in the country had left as well. Now they all began returning to Kuwait. The damage that had been inflicted during their absence was widespread and shocking.

77

When the cease-fire was announced, Iraqi soldiers departing Kuwait had deliberately bombed 732 of the country's 940 oil wells, setting 670 of them on fire. The country was literally ablaze; with about six million gallons of oil burning each day. Thick black smoke blocked the sun and filled the air. A Kuwaiti described the simple act of breathing as "like taking the exhaust pipe of a diesel truck in your mouth and breathing that." Another observer wrote, "Nothing in my experience compared to the eerie environment of the Burgan oil fields. . . . Though it was high noon, darkness had descended—the result of a black-gray oil cloud hanging permanently over the oil fields. . . . It was like the anteroom of hell, day become night. . . . "

The oil mist from the fires coated trees, making leaves shrivel and die. It also blackened the lungs of livestock, making people wonder anxiously about what it was doing to human lungs. As far away as Qatar, 400 miles to the south of Kuwait, and in Kashmir, 1,600 miles to the east, it rained black soot from these fires. Hospitals experienced a dramatic rise in respiratory cases, and pollution masks sold briskly for US$30 each at local supermarkets.

At first it was expected to take about two years to put out these fires and cap the oil spilling from the wells. But as the teams of expert firefighters from nations such as China, France, Hungary, and the United States worked, refining their techniques, the effort sped up tremendously. Still, it was dangerous work, with crews working near fires burning as hot as 480°F in the intense summer heat of Kuwait. The flames from the very last fire were finally doused by Sheik Jaber in a ceremony held in November 1991.

The fires and oil spills in the Persian Gulf also sparked a great deal of concern about the environment.

The chemicals from the oil might change the immune systems of fish and lead to cancer. Without healthy smaller fish to feed on, other marine life would die. The sticky consistency of the oil smothered birds and trapped other wildlife. Scientists also worried that the soot from the fires would disrupt the annual monsoon rains, and maybe even have an impact on global weather patterns.

In Kuwait City, the physical damage was just as devastating. There, departing Iraqi troops looted homes and office buildings, stealing televisions, computers, and whatever else they could find, loading everything into cars they had stolen for the purpose of escaping the country. The flight of Iraqis from Kuwait created an enormous traffic jam on a main road leading out of Kuwait City. To the surprise of Iraqi soldiers, and the horror of many observers, the United States launched a final bombing raid at this point, killing many of the flee-ing soldiers and leaving a long line of burnt-out cars and trucks along the road. This ghostly trail became known as the "Highway of Doom." Estimates of Iraqi casualties from this bombing ranged in the tens of thousands, although the Bush Administration refused to release its figures to the public.

The financial damage done to Kuwait was massive. During the occupation, the Iraqis had stolen more than $20 billion in gold and foreign currency. Roads, oil refineries, pipelines, and water desalination plants had also been badly damaged, along with widespread disruption of electrical and phone services. In Kuwait City, every bank, car dealership, hotel, store, and most office buildings had been torched. The beachfront was littered with the debris of war—wire, pillboxes (low concrete holders for machine guns), and mines. Saddam Hussein had also ordered his men to dump

Kuwaiti oil. Before evacuating the country, Iraqi soldiers managed to dump about 465 million gallons of crude oil into the water, killing more wildlife and wreaking havoc upon the environment in the Persian Gulf.

Many stories of horror emerged. When 21 professors at a Kuwaiti university refused to replace a picture of the emir with one of Hussein, they were brutally executed. Women and girls described being raped and mutilated, sometimes in front of their children or parents. It is estimated that thousands of Kuwaitis were tortured and murdered during this time.

The Iraqis also had systemically stripped the country of things of cultural value. The Sief Palace, home of the ruling family, was looted of irreplaceable pieces of Islamic art, as were Kuwaiti museums. "They tried to wipe out the identity of Kuwait, as if Kuwait did not exist," an Iraqi citizen commented.

At the national zoo, soldiers stole animals, transporting giraffes, monkeys, and elephants to the zoo in Baghdad. They also used caged animals for target practice, and when they grew hungry, they ate sheep, deer, and gazelles from the zoo.

As the government began rebuilding, they encouraged more Kuwaitis to work. Before the war, most of the country's manual laborers were foreigners. There were about 1.4 million non-Kuwaitis; of these about 350,000 were Palestinians, 200,000 were Egyptians, 500,000 were Asians, and a few were Europeans and Americans. Now the government wanted to cut back on the use of foreign technicians and unskilled laborers. This policy, known as "Kuwaitization," had actually begun before the war and was aimed at making sure that eventually two-thirds of the country's citizens would be Kuwaiti.

## INSTABILITY IN THE GULF

On April 6, 1991, the UN Security Council officially declared the end of the Persian Gulf War. In the cease-fire agreement, Iraq agreed to destroy all biological and chemical weapons; its facilities for producing such weapons; and any such materials or facilities it had for producing nuclear weapons. After the cease-fire, the UN continued the embargo against Iraq as a way of pressuring the country to carry out its agreements.

The signing of the cease-fire officially ended the war, but the threat from Saddam Hussein had not completely passed. President Bush had urged Iraqis to rebel against their leader. Now the Kurds in the northern part of the country staged rebellions, along with the Muslim Shiites in the south. The Iraqi army quickly quashed the revolts, forcing hundreds of thousands of Shiite Arabs to flee to Iran. Others hid in marshlands in southern Iraq. It is estimated that over a million Kurds fled to the mountainous terrain of northern Iraq and to other countries such as Iran and Turkey. Over 10,000 Kurds and Shiites were killed in the fighting or died of disease, exposure, or hunger.

In April the United States and the rest of the coalition created a safety zone in northern Iraq to protect Kurd refugees. Forces were stationed there until July.

In August 1992, to protect the Shiite population in southern Iraq, coalition forces also imposed a ban on Iraqi civilian and military aircraft flights over southern Iraq, making this a "no-fly" zone. The safety zone protecting the Kurds also included a ban on flights. Also in August, Saddam Hussein once again claimed that Kuwait was an Iraqi province. The UN Security Council responded to his claim by confirming the boundaries between Kuwait and Iraq as drawn by the Borders Committee.

Thousands of Kurdish refugees from Iraq came to this encampment on the Turkish-Iraqi border. They received military protection, housing, food, and medical care from a coalition of forces from around the world.

Tensions rose again in Kuwait in 1993 when Iraqi workers entered a demilitarized zone to retrieve Silkworm missiles they had left behind after the war. The United States and United Nations sent more security troops. Then Iraqi protestors threatened Kuwaitis who were digging a security trench along the border. When President Bush traveled to Kuwait, evidence of an assassination plot against him was uncovered. It was widely believed that Iraq was behind the plot.

In 1994, Hussein dispatched 20,000 more Iraqi troops to bolster the 50,000 regular troops stationed about 20 miles from the border. The UN condemned this Iraqi action, and the United States once again sent troops to Kuwait. However, despite these seemingly aggressive acts, Iraq insisted that it recognized Kuwait as a nation and was observing its borders.

In August 1994 fighting broke out among rival groups of Kurds in the safety zone. The Iraqi government sent troops and tanks into the zone to support one of the Kurdish groups. The United States opposed this and launched missiles against military targets in southern Iraq. The no-fly zone in southern Iraq was also expanded.

By 1995 the coalition was aware from satellite photos that Iraqis had seized over 9,000 items of military hardware during their occupation of Kuwait. This directly violated orders given by the UN. Two members of Hussein's family, who were now living in Jordan, added to the rising tensions when they revealed that another attack was being planned.

In 1996, Iraq launched missiles at two U.S. jets policing the no-fly zone. The U.S. president, Bill Clinton, dispatched F-117 Stealth fighters to Kuwait. Saddam Hussein immediately declared this an act of aggression on the part of Kuwait. The United States defended the move, saying that protection of Kuwait and Saudi Arabia was a part of American strategic interests.

## REBUILDING THE OIL INDUSTRY

The Kuwaiti government was attempting to rebuild its ruined country gainst this backdrop of political tension. Kuwaiti investments outside the country had provided funding for the expensive military action against Iraq. Upon the return of the emir and crown prince, construction began almost immediately to rebuild the devastated oil industry.

To help with the costly construction processes, the UN declared that Iraq would have to put a percentage of future oil revenues into a fund compensating victims of their invasion. Payouts from this fund were scheduled to begin in 1994.

While Kuwait was working to rebuild its petroleum industry, other Gulf States from the Gulf Cooperation Council—a security organization founded in 1981 by Kuwait, Saudi Arabia, the United Arab Emirates, Qatar, Oman, and Bahrain—produced oil on its behalf. Amazingly, by the end of 1992, the country's oil production was restored to 1.5 million barrels per day. Kuwait's current capacity is estimated at 2.5 million barrels per day. Depending upon market demand and OPEC agreements, the country plans to increase its capacity to 3.5 million barrels per day by 2005.

Much of the funding for the rebuilding came from money set aside from oil revenue. By law, 10 percent of Kuwaiti oil revenues must go into the Reserve Fund for Future Generations (RFFG). Before the war, this fund was worth an estimated $100 billion. By 1996 its worth had plummeted to $40 billion–50 billion.

The cost of the military defense of Kuwait in 1990–1991

totaled $22 billion. Rebuilding the country would cost another $20 billion. The Kuwaitis had no choice but to sell half the RFFG investments and borrow another $5.5 billion. The total cost of the Iraqi invasion to the country is estimated to be around $170 billion.

The Kuwaiti government realized it was essential to build up the military by bolstering training and buying new weapons. The government began making plans to reform the country's generous welfare system and cut back on public services. In addition, taxes on commercial and industrial profits were imposed and customs fees were hiked.

Damage to other industries was extensive as well. The Iraqis had looted all sorts of valuable high-tech machines at chemical plants and desalination plants, which needed to be replaced. Agriculture in Kuwait has always been limited by the dry desert terrain and lack of water. However, much of the soil in south central Kuwait, which previously had been arable, was destroyed when Iraqi troops set fire to oil wells.

## THE AL-SABAHS AFTER THE WAR

Despite the joyous celebrations that followed the liberation of Kuwait and the return of the emir, the al-Sabah family faced both criticism and social unrest after the war. Some Kuwaitis criticized the emir and his half-brother, the prime minister, for taking so long to return after the war. They had left Kuwait on the day of the invasion, August 2, 1990, and had not returned until March 14, 1991. Later they came under fire for establishing a lengthy and competitive bidding process by reviewing contracts for the recovery process, which significantly slowed the pace of the construction efforts.

Many Kuwaiti citizens were also outraged by the

A worker pauses for prayer near a burning oil field. Iraqi soldiers caused enormous damage by bombing oil wells as they retreated from Kuwait.

contrast between the emir's lifestyle upon his return and the struggles of ordinary citizens, whose day-to-day existence had become quite difficult, to say the least.

When the U.S. Army Corps of Engineers brought in the first truckload of supplies, about six days after the Iraqi defeat, the supplies did not consist of basics such as water, food, or badly needed electrical generators. Instead the truck was filled with luxurious new furnishings for one of the emir's palaces. The image of these nonessential things compounded bitter feelings created by the emir's taking so long to return to Kuwait.

Even American workers that were hired to restore one of the emir's palaces were surprised by the government's choice of priorities. With garbage lining the streets, little running water, scarce supplies of food, and limited phone service, refurnishing one of the emir's palaces struck one American, who was quoted in *The New Republic,* as a case of very bad judgment.

"It's sort of a values question," he commented. "You go out and see thousands of people in line to make a phone call and you come here [to the Bayan Palace] and see all this opulence and someone is complaining because there aren't enough gold fixtures."

The trauma of the war had also galvanized many people into demanding political change. Many Kuwaitis wanted greater participation in the reconvening of the National Assembly that was being planned for October. Kuwaitis also wanted to end the strict naturalization laws that restricted access to citizenship and voting rights. A minority was also demanding universal suffrage for women and a decrease in the voting age from 21 to 18. Adding to the sense of turmoil and uncertainty was an attack upon two proponents of democratic reform. Just three days after liberation, two opposition leaders involved in the push for greater democratic reforms, Hamad al-Jou'an and Hussein al-Bani, were shot by an unidentified Kuwaiti gunman. Al-Bani was killed, and al-Jou'an was paralyzed. Al-Jou'an's wife described it in *The Harvard International Review* as not just an attempt on their lives, "but an attempt to assassinate democracy." Despite the clamor for political change, however, most Kuwaitis still expressed support for the al-Sabah family.

In the days immediately following the liberation of Kuwait, chaos and unrest filled the streets. Emir Jaber imposed martial law when he returned to Kuwait. Despite his declaration that this would help to restore order, however, the opposite occurred. There was a wave of arrests, torture, and killings by Kuwaiti vigilantes and police. Most of these acts were aimed at foreigners.

At the time of the last census, Palestinians, Egyptians, Indians, Pakistanis, and Filipinos made up 60 percent of the population. Now there were bitter feelings toward these foreign groups, especially Palestinians. "The Palestinians who had lived here forty years, showed the Iraqis where all the prominent Kuwaitis lived," a woman living in Kuwait City told *The Harvard International Review.* "Then the Iraqis went to these homes and shot people in front of their homes."

Even though many Palestinians had stayed behind and even helped to defend Kuwait during the occupation, many Kuwaiti nationals blamed them for the country's plight. After the war, elaborate and discriminatory citizenship laws were established, and residents who did not meet the criteria were denied food and other relief. Noncitizens who had left the country during the war returned, only to find they were not allowed back in. Amnesty International, an organization that works to protect human rights worldwide, documented over 600 cases where people, mostly Palestinians, had been beaten, raped, tortured, and even executed, often by police.

The government fired most of the 110,000 Palestinian foreigners it had previously employed and began trying to restrict foreign domestic help hired by families and foreign workers hired by industry. But the new policy also brought back an old problem: Who would do the manual labor? Most Kuwaiti citizens were not about to take up many of the jobs that foreigners had filled for so long.

The war was over, but the al-Sabah family still had an enormous amount of work to do in healing its country.

Today Kuwait City is a busy center of trade and finance. These water towers (designed to look like minarets) overlook the city's coast on the bay in the Persian Gulf.

# 8

# Kuwait
# Today

Today Kuwait barely resembles the country that Mubarak the Great ruled at the turn of the 20th century. Tall skyscrapers dominate the horizon; new homes and office buildings have been constructed to accommodate the massive growth in industry; in the Persian Gulf, modern ships and oil tankers have replaced the sailing vessels of Mubarak's day. Kuwait's huge oil reserves have transformed the lives of many citizens and have had far-reaching consequences for both foreign and domestic policies.

Yet some things in Kuwait are quite the same. For example, Kuwaiti society today is layered much as it was when Mubarak ruled, with the al-Sabah at the top; the rich, influential merchants making up the second tier; natural-born Kuwaiti citizens on the next level; Arabs from other countries next; and finally all other foreigners. Sheik Mubarak might also recognize a familiar deference, a polite respect for authority that pervades Kuwaiti society. As heated as the discussions regarding democratic reform have become in the decade since the Persian Gulf War, most Kuwaitis continue to respect the members of the al-Sabah family, along with certain cultural traditions.

Mubarak would also find familiar his country's looking westward for defensive protection. Today the United States has a large role in policing the Middle East and monitoring Iraq's intentions toward Kuwait, much as Britain did at Mubarak's request in 1899 and into the 20th century. While Mubarak was trying to stave off a takeover by the Ottoman Turks, today's emir, Jaber al-Sabah III, has been forced to seek outside help in protecting his country from Iraq.

## DEMOCRATIC REFORM

After the Gulf War, the emir promised to reconvene the National Assembly. In October 1992 elections for a new National Assembly were held, with rather startling results. There were 278 candidates; the opposition candidates (not associated with the al-Sabah) won a whopping 30 of the body's 50 seats. Conservatives won 19 seats. Opposition members of Parliament won 6 of 16 positions in the cabinet, although the al-Sabah family held onto the important ministries of Defense, Foreign Affairs, and the Interior. In 1996 elections were held again, but under the laws of the time only 107,000 of Kuwait's 2 million residents were able to register to vote. Hundreds of women demonstrated at polling places, demanding the right to vote. In these 1996 elections, conservatives won fewer seats than they had won four years earlier.

On May 4, 1999, the emir once again dissolved the

National Assembly. However, new elections were held just two months later, on July 3, 1999, in keeping with the constitution.

There are no political parties in Kuwait, but there are several political groups that function like parties with different interests. These include the Islamic Constitutional Movement (Sunni Muslim and moderate); the Kuwait Democratic Forum (secular and liberal); Salafeen (Sunni Muslim and fundamentalist); the National Islamic Coalition (Shiite Muslim); and the Constitutional Group (merchants).

While the emir has the ultimate say in questions of policy, the Assembly is more involved in the process today, with the ability to generate legislation, question various ministries' administration, and even express a lack of confidence in ministers, which can require the minister to resign.

In May 1999 the emir issued several history-making decrees dealing with women's suffrage, economic liberalization, and nationality. However, the National Assembly later voted down all these decrees as a matter of principle, only to reintroduce the decrees themselves as parliamentary legislation.

The emir can ask the Assembly to reconsider proposed legislation. If the assembly passes it again by a two-thirds majority, however, then it becomes law. As happened after the Gulf War in 1991, the emir can declare martial law, but the Assembly must approve it. The National Assembly meets for at least eight months of the year.

The country's judicial system was adopted in 1960. Today there are six kinds of courts for resolving different cases: Constitutional Court, Court of Cassation (verdicts from the Court of Appeal and the State Security Court); Court of Appeal; Court of First Instance; Summary Court; and Traffic Court.

After the Gulf War, Kuwaiti courts had to deal with matters related to the occupation. A Martial Law Tribunal handled cases involving people accused of collaborating with the Iraqis. In 1994, when the assassination plot against President George H.W. Bush was uncovered, a panel of three judges presided over a long trial. Finally, five Iraqis and one Kuwaiti were sentenced to death by hanging. Seven others received 6 months to 12 years jail time. During the process, there were complaints that torture was a common means of getting confessions.

## THE ROLE OF WOMEN

While Kuwaiti women enjoy more freedom and privileges than they do elsewhere in the Gulf States, by Western standards there is still much progress to be made. Two of the most contentious issues today are women's rights to vote and to run for political office. In 1999, Sheik Jaber III issued a royal decree granting women the right to vote, along with the right to hold office. However, the National Assembly voted down the measure in November 1999, claiming that the time was not right for granting these rights.

While many Kuwaitis interpret Islam as forbidding women to hold positions of authority, Islamic law actually states that all people are equal under the law. Other Kuwaitis believe that women vote through their fathers and husbands, who cast a vote for their entire family.

While so far denied the right to vote and to hold office, women have been increasingly politically active in recent years. During the Gulf War, women's groups protested the Iraqi occupation. Women have also protested government policy by constant marches on the National Assembly and into voter registration centers in police stations. Influential social and cultural groups such as the Women Affairs Committee and Kuwait's Union of Women Societies, along with international women's groups, have also given Kuwaiti women a voice in political affairs.

With women continuing to pressure the government for reform, it seems likely that they will be granted the right to vote before the next elections. However, some women fear that they will continue to be denied the right to run for political office, a "compromise" decided upon by the members of Parliament.

Unlike those of other Muslim nations, Kuwaiti women do have access to education. Education for females started in 1937. When Kuwait University opened in 1966, women quickly became the majority, comprising over 60 percent of the student body. Today, over 67 percent of Kuwait University graduates are women. An estimated 34 percent of the total labor force is female— the highest percentage in the Persian Gulf region. Women hold a wide range of positions, from jobs in the oil industry to employment in research, education, and medicine. Some older Kuwaitis object to women working at all, believing instead that women belong at home, raising a family.

Women are allowed to dress as they like; however, their attire also remains the subject of debate. Many conservative Muslims want to make traditional dress, a long black robe and veil, mandatory. Others believe that traditional attire should be banned from the university and public offices. Some women wear veils that partially cover their face, although for safety reasons, full veils have been officially banned while driving. Contact with Westerners, as well as with conservative Saudi Arabians, during the Gulf War reignited the debate over dress— and over many other aspects of Muslim life. In response to greater exposure to Western cultures, more Kuwaiti women wear the traditional robe and veil than did before the Gulf War.

## RELIGION

The majority of Kuwaitis are Muslims. Their identity as Muslims remains strong, guiding all aspects of life, including political decisions.

Muslims adhere to the five pillars, or requirements, of the faith: profession of faith; praying five times daily; giving alms; fasting during the month of Ramadan; and making a pilgrimage to Mecca at least once in a lifetime. Prayers are offered almost anywhere, sometimes even in the street, and are uttered in Arabic, while facing Mecca. Most Kuwaitis carry alarm clocks or special watches with compasses that indicate prayer times, along with the direction of Mecca.

Most Kuwaitis are Sunni Muslims. However, the Shiites form a significant minority, about 25 percent of the population. Both Sunnis and Shiites serve in the Kuwaiti government.

Mosques for Muslim worship are found in nearly all public buildings. The mosques are oriented toward Mecca and used as places for instruction and meeting, as well as prayer and meditation. Women are given separate rooms in mosques so that men will not see them.

Conservative Kuwaitis continue to wrestle with other groups that find ways to reconcile modern practices with Islamic tradition. This struggle has heated up in the years since the Gulf War, in which Westerners played such a large role. This struggle is reflected especially in the intensity of the debate regarding women's rights.

There is a small group of Christians in Kuwait, and they are treated with tolerance. Christianity began to be practiced in Kuwait in the early 1900s, with the arrival of American missionaries. The oil boom further attracted foreigners to the country. The constitution protects the freedom to practice religions other than Islam, and the Kuwaiti government officially recognizes three principal Christian churches: the Evangelical Church of Kuwait, the Roman Catholic Church, and the Roman Orthodox Church. There are about 200 Kuwaiti Christian families and many more Christian expatriates.

Kuwait has maintained unusually strong relations with the Vatican. In 1996 it became the first Persian Gulf nation to receive a top Vatican official. And Kuwait is the only member of the Gulf Cooperation Council to maintain diplomatic relations with the Vatican State.

## OIL AND INDUSTRY

Despite the widespread damage to the oil infrastructure by Iraq, Kuwait currently has the capacity to produce 2.5 million barrels of oil per day. This surpasses the 1.5 million barrel level of 1990, before the Iraqi invasion. The speed in which the oil industry has recovered from the Gulf War has been remarkable.

Over the years, investment abroad has become extremely important to the Kuwaiti economy and the future. After oil, investment is the second biggest source of revenue for the country. In some ways Kuwait functions like an international corporation—its strategy being to diversify its assets and financial base away from oil, to protect itself from a future without oil reserves. Kuwait currently has ownership in foreign banks and insurance companies, and it has massive real estate holdings in the United States and Europe. It has shares in many Fortune 500 companies and is rumored to be the largest single foreign investor in the Tokyo stock market. When Iraq invaded Kuwait in 1990, Kuwait was reportedly earning $6 trillion annually from stocks, bank holdings, and real estate. Its diverse investment holdings also provided much of the funding for the country's enormous reconstruction costs. These holdings allowed the country to stay afloat during

Kuwait continues to be a major supplier of oil, with the goal of producing 3.5 million barrels of oil per day by the year 2005.

the war, in spite of the chaos and massive looting that went on. The government's two reserve funds—the Reserve Fund for Future Generations and the General Reserve Fund—dropped to about $40 billion after the war. Today they are estimated at about $80 billion. Most of this reserve is invested in the United States, Germany, the United Kingdom, Japan, France, and Southeast Asia.

Kuwait continues to provide economic assistance to other states, primarily through the Kuwait Fund for Arab Economic Development. Initially founded to fund other Arab countries, in 1974, it expanded its agenda to include non-Arab developing nations in need. Over the years aid has been given to Egypt, Syria, Jordan, the PLO, and even Iraq, during the Iran–Iraq War. During the fiscal year ending in

June 2000, the fund issued loans and technical assistance grants totaling $520 million.

Other industries have been restored to their prewar capabilities as well. Industry in Kuwait today consists of several large petrochemical companies, oil refineries, and a range of smaller manufacturers. There are water desalination plants as well as ammonia, desulfurization, fertilizer, brick, block, and cement plants. New equipment in these plants has replaced the old machines looted by the Iraqis.

Although the soil that was most suitable for farming was destroyed by oil fires during the war, there is a small agriculture industry in Kuwait. The government has experimented with growing food hydroponically (in nutrient-rich solutions of sand, water, and plant food) and on closely managed farms. Commercial fishing has been developed in territorial waters, where there is an abundance of fish and shrimp, and in the Indian Ocean.

The Kuwait Oil Tankers Company has 35 crude oil and refined product carriers. It is the largest tanker company in an OPEC country.

## FOREIGN AFFAIRS

Since the Gulf War, Kuwait has focused on developing and maintaining relations with countries that were part of the coalition that liberated the country from the Iraqi invasion. These countries were given opportunities to receive contracts for the long and expensive reconstruction effort in Kuwait.

Kuwait's relationship with Iraq remains tense. At a 2002 Arab summit in Lebanon, Kuwait claimed that Iraq was still holding at least 600 Kuwaiti citizens. Kuwait demanded that these people be released or accounted for. Iraq in turn claimed that Kuwait was holding Iraqi citizens—a charge denied by Kuwait's government. Faced with other Arab leaders attempting to help the two countries reconcile, Kuwait's minister of state for foreign affairs said that "reconciliation efforts" have been hurt by an Iraqi refusal to offer guarantees that it will not attack Kuwait again.

Relations with countries that supported Iraq during the war, such as Jordan, Sudan, Yemen, and Cuba, also remain strained. Because of PLO Chairman Yasir Arafat's support of Saddam Hussein during the occupation, Kuwait's relationship with the PLO has grown colder, too. Out of necessity, Kuwait has concluded defense arrangements with the United States, Russia, the United Kingdom, and France and maintained close relationships with members of the UN Security Council. Kuwait also has maintained strong relationships with Egypt and Syria.

Since the war, Kuwait has attempted to increase the size of its armed forces and update its equipment. The United States has provided military and defensive assistance through the sale of equipment and training.

## THE FUTURE

Emir Jaber III still rules Kuwait. However, he is in his 70s, and the crown prince, Saad, has been ill for years, so many of his responsibilities have been fulfilled by a deputy. No matter who succeeds them, the next generation of al-Sabah sheiks, along with the National Assembly, is sure to continue wrestling with the following political tensions in Kuwaiti society: how much power to give to the National Assembly; whether to grant more rights to women; and how to redefine the role of the al-Sabahs in governing the country. As Kuwaitis continue to be exposed to Western cultures and values, more questions about living in an Islamic society will arise. Conservative fundamentalists will continue pressing for the preservation of old customs and traditions, while more moderate Muslims will seek to find ways to incorporate new freedoms and cultural change.

Future emirs and members of the National Assembly will continue to struggle with questions of foreign labor as well. Young Kuwaitis have been encouraged to work, especially in the private sector. However, in 2001 unemployment in Kuwait rose to an unprecedented 2.5 percent. For the first time, the government has not been able to provide public service jobs for nationals looking for employment.

In recent years, the divisions between the Arab and non-Arab worlds have been sharpened by the events of September 11, 2001, when terrorists attacked the World Trade Towers in New York City and the Pentagon building outside Washington, DC. Escalating violence in Israel between the Jews and Palestinians in 2002 further defined these divisions and forced Kuwait to reexamine yet again its relationships with the West and the rest of the Arab world. When the United States claimed in 2002 that Saddam Hussein continued to pose a threat to world security, and expressed interest in launching a military strike against him, Kuwait reacted cautiously. Kuwait is keenly aware of the instability that already exists in the Middle East. The Kuwaiti government did not want to rock what was already a very unstable boat.

While many aspects of the future remain uncharted, for now the story of Kuwait is basically a success story. The country has achieved enviable financial success by distributing much of its wealth, diversifying its investment holdings overseas, and diversifying industry as much as possible at home. The country also has managed to repair the damage inflicted by the Iraqis in record time and to grant its citizens some democratic reforms. Most consistently throughout its history, Kuwait has managed to cling fiercely to its independence and national identity in the face of numerous and formidable challenges. Certainly Mubarak al-Sabah would recognize this indomitable Kuwaiti spirit.

| | |
|---|---|
| **1716** | Tribal people from Arabian Desert migrate to Kuwait. |
| **1756** | First ruler of Kuwait, Sheik Sabah I, chosen. |
| **1896** | Sheik Mubarak seizes power from Muhammad and Jarrah al-Sabah. |
| **1899** | Sheik Mubarak signs the Exclusive Agreement, the secret defensive treaty with British. |
| **1914** | World War I breaks out in Europe. |
| **1915** | Mubarak the Great dies; Jaber II succeeds him. |
| **1917** | Sheik Salim succeeds Jaber II. |
| **1921** | Sheik Ahmad succeeds Salim. |
| **1922** | Conference of Uqair held to negotiate boundaries among Kuwait, Saudi Arabia, and Iraq. |
| **1934** | Joint concession granted to Gulf Oil of the United States and Anglo Persian Oil of Great Britain for deep drilling. |
| **1936** | Deep drilling begins. |
| **1938** | Majlis Movement organized by Kuwaiti merchants. |
| **1942** | Oil wells plugged until the end of World War II. |
| **1946** | First barrel of oil exported. |
| **1950** | Sheik Abdullah III succeeds Ahmad. |
| **1961** | Kuwait becomes an independent state in June. Joins the Arab League in July. |
| **1962** | The Constitution of Kuwait is ratified. |
| **1963** | In January, Kuwait holds first parliamentary elections. Kuwait joins the United Nations in May. |
| **1965** | Sheik Sabah III succeeds Abdullah III. |
| **1967** | Six-Day War between the Arabs and Israelis. Kuwait joins oil embargo against countries supporting Israel. |
| **1977** | Sheik Jaber III, the present day emir, succeeds Sheik Sabah III. |
| **1979** | Ruhollah Khomeini becomes new leader of Iran. |
| **1980** | Iraq invades Iran, sparking the Iran-Iraq War. |
| **1985** | Sheik Jaber III dissolves the National Assembly, citing security. |

**1988**   Iran-Iraq War ends.

**1990**   Iraq invades Kuwait on August 2.

**1991**   Allies launch Operation Desert Storm on January 17 at 3 A.M. Kuwait is declared liberated on February 26.

**1992**   New Legislative Assembly elected.

**1996**   Elections for National Assembly held again.

**1999**   National Assembly dissolved by the emir in May. New elections held in July.

Allen, Thomas B., Clifton F. Berry, and Norman Polmar, editors. *War in the Gulf: From the Invasion of Kuwait to the Day of Victory and Beyond*. New York: Turner Publishing, 1991.

Armstrong, Karen. *Islam: A Short History*. New York: Random House, 2000.

Bratsman, Fred. *War in the Persian Gulf*. Brookfield, Connecticut: Millbrook Press, 1991.

Crystal, Jill. *Kuwait: The Transformation of an Oil State*. San Francisco, California: Westview Press, 1992.

Foster, Leila Merrel. *Kuwait*. Danbury, Connecticut: Children's Press, 1998.

Hoad, Al, and Abdul Latif. *Islam*. New York: Bookwright Press, 1987.

Hourani, Albert. *A History of the Arab Peoples*. New York: Warner Books, 1992.

**WEBSITES:**

*www.arab.net*

*www.embassyofkuwait.com*

*www.kuwait-info.org*

*www.kuwaitonline.com*

*www.radiokuwait.org*

Ajami, Fouad. *The Dream Palace of the Arabs: A Generation's Odyssey.* New York: Vintage Books, 1998.

Allen, Thomas B., Clifton F. Berry, and Norman Polmar, editors. *War in the Gulf: From the Invasion of Kuwait to the Day of Victory and Beyond.* New York: Turner Publishing, 1991.

Armstrong, Karen. *Islam: A Short History.* New York: Random House, 2000.

Bennis, Phyllis and Michel Moushabeck, editors. *Beyond the Storm: A Gulf Crisis Reader.* Brooklyn, New York: Olive Branch Press, 1991.

Foster, Leila Merrel. *Kuwait.* Danbury, Connecticut: Children's Press, 1998.

Hourani, Albert. *A History of the Arab Peoples.* New York: Warner Books, 1992.

Huffman, Karen Kirk. *Living the Nightmare: Escape from Kuwait.* Lincoln, Nebraska: Dageforde Publishing, 1999.

Sasson, Jean P. *The Rape of Kuwait: The True Story of Iraqi Atrocities Against a Civilian Population.* New York: Knightsbridge Publishing Company, 1991.

David, Peter. *Triumph in the Desert: A Commemorative Photo History of the Gulf War.* New York: Random House, 1991.

**WEBSITES :**

*www.arab.net*

*www.kuwaitonline.com*

*www.kuwait-info.org*

**SUSAN KORMAN** is the author of more than 20 books for young readers, including picture books, series fiction, and several biographies. Formerly a children's book editor at several publishing companies, she currently works as a freelance writer and is studying to become a school librarian. While Susan has never visited Kuwait, she enjoyed learning more about this Persian Gulf nation as well as the rest of the Middle East. She lives in Yardley, Pennsylvania, with her husband and three children, two cats, and one dog.

**AKBAR S. AHMED** holds the Ibn Khaldun Chair of Islamic Studies at the School of International Service of American University. He is actively involved in the study of global Islam and its impact on contemporary society. He is the author of many books on contemporary Islam, including *Discovering Islam: Making Sense of Muslim History and Society,* which was the basis for a six-part television program produced by the BBC called *Living Islam.* Ahmed has been a visiting professor and the Stewart Fellow in the Humanities at Princeton University, as well as a visiting professor at Harvard University and Cambridge University.